The Liquid Plain

The Liquid Plain is published by Theatre Communications Group, Inc., 520 Eighth Avenue, 24th Floor, New York, NY 10018-4156

Page 37, 93: "The Chimney Sweeper" by William Blake, *Songs of Innocence*, 1789. Page 39: "America: A Prophecy" by William Blake, 1793. Page 96: "All Religions Are One" by William Blake, 1788; "The Clod and the Pebble" by William Blake, *Songs of Experience*, 1794. Page 121: "A Divine Image" by William Blake, *Songs of Experience*, 1794.

The publication of *The Liquid Plain* by Naomi Wallace, through TCG's Book Program, is made possible in part by the New York State Council on the Arts with the support of Governor Andrew Cuomo and the New York State Legislature.

TCG books are exclusively distributed to the book trade by Consortium Book Sales and Distribution.

LIBRARY OF CONGRESS CATALOGING-IN-PUBLICATION DATA

Wallace, Naomi, author.
The liquid plain / Naomi Wallace.
First edition.
ISBN 9781559365147 (softcover)
ISBN 9781559368414 (ebook)
DDC 812/.54—dc23

Cover design, book design and composition by Lisa Govan
Cover art by Bruce McLeod

First Edition, August 2016

This play is for my three daughters,
Nadira, Caitlin and Tegan,
and for Bruce. Always.

Contents

Special Thanks

This play would not have come into being without the brilliant works of Robin D. G. Kelley and Marcus Rediker.

The watery world in this play is for Ellen Gallagher, an underwater visionary, whose portholes give us dangerous and daring insight.

Rediker's magnificent book, *The Slave Ship: A Human History* (2007), resurrected him.

And yet, in both cases "actual events" mask deeper, more fundamental truths.

The African-born Wheatley, early America's most famous poet, took off for "Britannia's distant shore" partly to improve her health, partly to seek out a publisher. Paradoxically, she traveled in the company of her slave master's son, Nathaniel Wheatley. In other words, she was property. The poem's apparent nostalgia for New England veils her recognition that the England of old had just become liberated territory for the enslaved. A year prior to her journey, a fugitive from slavery named James Somerset successfully sued for his right to freedom in the British high court. Chief Justice Lord Mansfield ruled that because England never passed a law legalizing slavery, masters could not force fugitives back into slavery as long as they were on English soil. So when Wheatley writes in the same poem, "But thou! Temptation hence away / With all thy fatal train / Nor once seduce my soul away," it is not clear whether she is speaking of England or America—the former, the temptation to seize her freedom; the latter, the temptation to return home without it. Either way, we know it was on her mind when she penned "A Farewell to America," however camouflaged behind flowery verse. We also know that she returned to New England a slave, choosing to negotiate her freedom over a fugitive life in the sanctuary of Britannia. She was finally freed upon the death of her master, John Wheatley, in 1778, and she herself died six years later at the age of thirty-one, broken and penniless.

In *The Liquid Plain*, reversing sail across the Atlantic also serves as a possible path to freedom. The rough, cold waters first experienced as the nightmare of the Middle

Passage—young men, women and children packed tightly into dark cargo holds, chained together, suffering from dysentery, fever, malnutrition and brutality—appeared as the dream of returning home. Except that Wallace's characters chose fugitivity, self-liberation, and Africa over the kindness of white men, the fairness of white law, and the paternalism of England. Indeed, she succeeds in transforming a tale of white bourgeois villainy and white working-class courage into a story that centers on the struggles of black women for freedom and justice.

Set in Bristol, Rhode Island, the first act takes place in 1791, the year of De Wolfe's trial and the first year of the Haitian Revolution—the massive slave insurrection that not only destroyed slavery on the island but established the first independent black nation in the Western Hemisphere. Act One opens with two lovers, Adjua and Dembi, fugitives from slavery, hustling along Bristol's docks with dreams of returning to West Africa and raising a free child on soil they can call home. As they await passage on a ship captained by a former slave named Liverpool Joe, they pull what they think is a corpse from the water in search of valuables. The man turns out to be John Cranston—still alive but temporarily devoid of memory. Thus begins a journey that defies summary, whose tragic and prophetic twists and turns can only be experienced on the stage or in the pages that follow.

Suffice it to say, Adjua does bear a child, a girl named Bristol, who appears in Act Two and Act Three as a forty-six-year-old woman. The year is 1837, three decades after the abolition of the slave trade and three years after the abolition of slavery in the British Empire. She makes the transatlantic voyage to the Rhode Island port city for which she was named, but from England, not Africa. And the point of her journey was not to seek freedom—at least not at first—but to exact justice. In the brilliant and determined Bristol Waters, the former slaver-turned-senator James De Wolfe will face his reckoning. And in Bristol's own reckoning with history, death, Africa, ancestors, and the ghost of poet William Blake, she will discover her calling. Bristol's dialogue with De Wolfe is a veritable masterpiece, a brilliant exposé of the conceits of Enlightenment-era civilization that transmuted people into cargo and capital, that made murder an economic calculation, that cloaked the bloody business of human trafficking in the refined garments of humanitarianism, and that built a paradise from the bones, sinew and sweat of African people. Bristol strips De Wolfe and the entire system naked, exposing his/its true identity: Butcher. Executioner. Criminal.

Wallace's brilliance is her ability to reveal the system of modern slavery, its consequences and contradictions, without ever representing *slaves*, the Middle Passage, or the brutal operations of the plantation. While the play stays anchored in the lives and struggles of black women seeking freedom and justice, Wallace is sensitive to the ways in which slavery pulled everyone into its bloody fold: Europeans and Africans, children and adults, women and men, the rich and the dispossessed. Inevitably, a system of industrial-scale kidnapping bound together the Atlantic world—a world comprised of Africans escaping bondage, sailors resisting impressment, laboring women fighting concubinage, masters and owners and managers wrestling with their own dehumanization.

And yet, Wallace avoids the lure of "equivalency," of treating impressed sailors or the suppressed European laborers as equally oppressed by the Atlantic slave system. John Cranston is neither a hero nor the star of the story—yes, he is victimized, but he is also a victimizer. Likewise, Dembi, Adjua, Liverpool Joe and Bristol are never victims—indeed, they are never slaves. Wallace grasped what most historians have yet to understand: that slaves only existed in the white imagination, and that the African refused to become a "slave"—which is to say a saleable, docile commodity ready and willing to create surplus for her owner. On the contrary, they were the system's executioners, soldiers of liberty whose hatred of bondage and love of humanity drove them to act, often constructively but sometimes destructively.

So get ready. Batten down the hatches. Throw all assumptions overboard. And prepare for a voyage that will leave you astonished, edified, and at times utterly breathless.

The
Liquid Plain

Production History

The world premiere of *The Liquid Plain* was produced by Oregon Shakespeare Festival (Bill Rauch, Artistic Director; Cynthia Rider, Executive Director) in Ashland, Oregon, on July 2, 2013. It was directed by Kwame Kwei-Armah. The scenic design was by Brenda Davis, the costume design was by Constanza Romero, the lighting design was by Christopher Akerlind, the sound design and original music were by Victoria Deiorio and the projection and video design were by Alex Koch; the dramaturg was Julie Felise Dubiner and the stage manager was D. Christian Bolender. The cast was:

ADJUA	June Carryl
DEMBI	Kimberly Scott
CRANSTON	Danforth Comins
BALTHAZAR/WILLIAM BLAKE	Armando Durán
LIVERPOOL JOE	Kevin Kenerly
BRISTOL	Bakesta King
JAMES DE WOLFE	Michael Winters
NESBITT	Josiah Phillips
GIFFORD	Richard Elmore
ENSEMBLE	June Carryl, Kevin Kenerly

The New York premiere of *The Liquid Plain* was produced by Signature Theatre (James Houghton, Artistic Director; Erika Mallin, Executive Director) on March 8, 2015. It was directed by Kwame Kwei-Armah. The scenic design was by Riccardo Hernandez, the costume design was by Paul Tazewell, the lighting design was by Thom Weaver, the sound design and original music were by Shane Rettig and the projection design was by Alex Koch; the production stage manager was Cole P. Bonenberger. The cast was:

ADJUA	Kristolyn Lloyd
DEMBI	Ito Aghayere
CRANSTON	Michael Izquierdo
BALTHAZAR/WILLIAM BLAKE	Karl Miller
LIVERPOOL JOE	Johnny Ramey
BRISTOL	LisaGay Hamilton
JAMES DE WOLFE	Robert Hogan
NESBITT	Lance Roberts
GIFFORD	Tuck Milligan
THE SHADOW	Tara A. Nicolas

The role of Bristol was originally written for LisaGay Hamilton.

Characters

ADJUA, born in West Africa, early twenties

DEMBI, born into slavery, from Charleston, mid-twenties

CRANSTON, a white sailor, born in American Colonies, early thirties

BALTHAZAR, Irish, United Irishman, thirties

LIVERPOOL JOE, a black sailor, grew up in Liverpool, twenties

BRISTOL, a free black woman, grew up in England, forties

WILLIAM BLAKE, the poet

JAMES DE WOLFE, a former U.S. senator, seventies

NESBITT, an old black sailor

GIFFORD, an old white sailor

THE SHADOW, a presence, the spirit of Adjua's sister

GUINEA WORMS

Time

A possible 1791, and 1837.

Places

A harsh, dangerous and imagined Bristol, Rhode Island.

Docks. Tavern. Library of a grand estate. Bottom of the ocean.

Notes

Accents should be light, just a touch, and not realistic. As though remembered from another time.

This is a world conjured from imagination. Nothing about the design needs to be historically accurate.

In the Signature Theatre production, the text of each "passage" was projected for a few moments at the beginning of each scene.

While for Britannia's distant shore
We weep the liquid plain,
And with astonish'd eyes explore
The wide-extended main.

—PHILLIS WHEATLEY
"A FAREWELL TO AMERICA," 1773

Prelude

Bristol, Rhode Island, 1791. The far end of the docks. Between the dark and daybreak. As the lights come up, we see The Shadow sprinkle something like powder around the stage. The Shadow then disappears. Now we see Adjua helping Dembi wrap and hide Dembi's breasts with a long, narrow piece of cloth. This is a ritual between them, and it is both sensual and simple. There are a few moments of wrapping and silence between them. Adjua gives her words to Dembi like a prayer. What they say to one another is a part of the morning ritual, a preparation for the day.

ADJUA: My love. *(Beat)* When we find our way back home, we will make our child together. It will be the most beautiful child.

DEMBI: Yes he will.

ADJUA: And this child'll be a hundred worlds rising.

DEMBI: Our miracle.

(Dembi pulls on his shirt, adjusts it. Now they are both ready to face whatever the day brings.)

Act One

Scene One

Projected Text: Book One. Passage of Clay: Bristol, Rhode Island, 1791.

The docks. We hear ships rubbing against the docks, water rolling, though the sound is slightly distorted and not realistic.

We now see empty sugar casks. A pile of old rope. A heap of torn sails still needing to be mended. Perhaps a broken mast off the dock, the rusty chain of an anchor or a piece of severed hull. Sharp, dangerous things. And yet the docks are not cluttered. This part of the dock, though now mostly bare and derelict, was once busy with the small industry of the poor.

This is a world of violence and the threat of violence. There is always the presence of danger, and the decisiveness of people to use brute force, and respond to it. It is a predatory, ferocious environment with ragged edges that cut at every turn.

Lights up on Adjua and Dembi leaning over a jagged hole in the dock, clutching the legs of a drowned man that they are pulling out of the water, feet first.

At all times, Dembi and Adjua take care not to be seen, on the docks or anywhere else, though this vigilance has become natural to them now. However, the fact that they are in hiding is not at first clearly evident to us or others. Both are highly intelligent thinkers, though in different ways. Adjua is intent on mapping out their ambitions, though her exertions diminish neither her spark nor her passion. She walks with a slight limp but this does not keep her from being light on her feet and vigorous. Dembi is tough, suspicious, a steely eyed survivor ready to take ruthless action when danger appears. His focus is on Adjua and their daily survival. They are passionately in love with one another, though they keep a lid on it because of daily brute realities. Most of the time, the characters onstage are engaged in some kind of industry, be it mending, sharpening or assembling.

DEMBI: Heave. Heave!
ADJUA: Pull!
DEMBI: Damn, he's full of water.
ADJUA: Trekken!
DEMBI: Come on out, you rake.
ADJUA: Mijn Got, he's a fat one!
DEMBI: And this one still got his clothes.
ADJUA: Nee let him slip.
DEMBI: We get the knave in.

(They pull the body onto the dock. The body is face down. Adjua pulls at the cloth on the body's bottom.)

Not a bad cloth.

ADJUA: Ja. Something fine I sew up with this!
DEMBI: What's here?

(Dembi digs in the man's seat pocket and finds a small, wet book. They both stare at it. Then Adjua grabs it.)

A book.
ADJUA: A reading man.
DEMBI: Give't here. I found it.
ADJUA: I found the body. But we can share, ja.
DEMBI: We dry it out. Get a coin for it.
ADJUA: Let's turn him over.

(They roll him onto his back.)

DEMBI: Not been long in the water.
ADJUA: Still got a face.
DEMBI: There's a knot on his head, there. Clothes off, fast.
ADJUA: Ja. Before someone come and take him from us, like the last one.

(As they speak, Dembi and Adjua proceed to strip the body down to its underwear. This is done with such precision and care, in tandem, that we're sure it's not the first time.)

DEMBI: Don't tear the vest. It's got buttons.
ADJUA: Of bone. A landlubber for sure.
DEMBI: Big feet like me. The shoes are mine.
ADJUA: Nee, love. We sell it all but the book.
DEMBI: You keep the book. I keep the shoes.
ADJUA: Dembi!
DEMBI: I'll wear them for a little while. Dry them out. Then we'll sell 'em.

ADJUA: Promise?
DEMBI: Sure. Check his grinders.

(They examine the dead man's teeth.)

You make some dentures?
ADJUA: Not going to be easy. He got a few left but deep roots.

(Adjua holds the man's face gently in her hands and wonders as to his story. Dembi watches jealously.)

We seen his face before . . . ?
DEMBI: The drowned all look the same. Don't touch his face like that.
ADJUA: By his look I see he suffer hard. Poor man.

(Adjua loses her hold when Dembi picks up the man's feet and begins to drag him back to the hole in the dock.)

What you doing?

(Adjua again grabs the body. They both pull at it.)

DEMBI: We got his clothes; we throw him back in the water.
ADJUA: Nee be a sinner, Dembi, or he'll bring us bad luck.
DEMBI: If we didn't spy him, he still be in his watery grave!
ADJUA: We got to bury him proper so his spirit be happy and leave us alone.
DEMBI: But if the constable and watch come, they blame us and we're dead.

(Dembi pulls at the body.)

ADJUA: I won't let you do it. A dead man is a brother in need.
DEMBI: A brother is a man who look like me.
ADJUA: Don't go to hell.

(Dembi stops pulling.)

DEMBI: You don't believe in no hell.
ADJUA: We got to wrap and bury him.
DEMBI: Can't take the risk. We throw the wretch back in.

(Dembi pulls harder.)

ADJUA: I won't let you do it, you bastard.

(The curses they throw at one another are sharp but have a playful edge.)

DEMBI: Bastard now, am I? You're nothing but a saltwater slave, let go.
ADJUA: Least I born in Africa. *(Beat)* Blackamoor. Mungo.
DEMBI: Coromantee bitch.
ADJUA: Yes. And this Coromantee still a warrior, you slave you. You poor excuse for an Igbo.
DEMBI: The Igbo have no king. That's what we say.
ADJUA: But I am your queen. Teef. Lieverd. Rot zak. Schofter.
DEMBI: I like it when you curse me in Dutch . . . Let go!

(Dembi and Adjua pull and heave the body, each intent on winning their way, until suddenly the body opens its eyes and screams loud enough to make them drop him. Silence. They each stare at one another.)

ADJUA: Ja. Okay. We throw him back in and quick.

(Cranston retches and throws up water.)

DEMBI: I'm not returning the shoes.
ADJUA: Or the book, nee.
DEMBI: Or the vest.
ADJUA: Maybe he's dead and just pretending.
DEMBI: Or a spirit's moving his bones.
ADJUA: Or Papa Legba's inside him with a trick in his gut.
DEMBI: Thin like a breath, the wall 'tween living and dead. *(To Cranston)* Are you awake or a spirit?

(Cranston is too bewildered to speak.)

Eyes too stupid to be a spirit.
ADJUA *(To Cranston)*: Can you speak?

(No answer. Dembi and Adjua get a bit closer.)

You want us to throw you in the water again?

(After a moment, Cranston understands and he's scared.)

CRANSTON: No. No. I'm cold. Please. Cold.
DEMBI *(Teasing)*: Mustn't go about naked then.

(Cranston feels the bump on his head.)

CRANSTON: My head hurts.
DEMBI: Who are you, man?
CRANSTON: My name is . . . They call me . . .
ADJUA: They call you . . . ?

(Cranston doesn't know. Then something comes to him.)

CRANSTON: The. Hogs.
DEMBI: Thehogs?
CRANSTON: My toes! The hogs picked 'em clean while he slept and then his toes were little stick bones.

(Cranston clutches his toes, but then sees they are intact. He retches again.)

DEMBI: I don't think the suit's his. Or the book. Most likely a thief for sure.
CRANSTON: I'm a thief! *(Beat)* I'm a thief?
ADJUA: What did you steal?
CRANSTON: I stole. I stole.

(He now looks down at his half nakedness and seems to understand it.)

My clothes. Some badger stole my clothes! Help, help me!

(Dembi puts a knife to Cranston's throat.)

DEMBI: Holler again and I'll stick you.

(Cranston is too weak to resist. Dembi releases him.)

ADJUA: Just what was you wearing then, Lieverd?
DEMBI: Don't call him lieverd. You only call me—
CRANSTON: Lieverd?
ADJUA *(To Dembi)*: Ja, Sweetheart. Hush up. *(To Cranston)* What was you wearing?
CRANSTON: I was wearing. A. Two. Something . . .
ADJUA: If you can't remember then it can't be thief'd.

DEMBI: I remember. He was wearing . . . a sail. You were wearing a sail! Adjua, fetch it back.

(Adjua catches on. She gets a dirty, old piece of sail. Dembi quickly slices some holes in it, then throws it to Cranston.)

There's your clothes back.

(Cranston looks doubtful but then puts the sail cloth on. But he's got nothing to tie it with.)

CRANSTON: Got a spare piece of rope?
DEMBI: You just keep taking, don't you?

(Dembi throws him a piece of rope. Cranston ties it around his waist.)

CRANSTON: I hear a tail flappin'. There's a fish in my ear.

(Cranston tries to dislodge the fish he thinks is in his ear by hitting the side of his head, and as he does so, his eyes alight on Adjua.)

A pretty one you are, so pretty and—
DEMBI *(Interrupts)*: Your name.

(He doesn't know. Adjua makes up a name.)

ADJUA: Jeffrey.
CRANSTON: Jeffrey?
DEMBI: Sinker. Sure. Jeffrey Sinker. Why not?
CRANSTON: I don't feel like a Jeffrey Sink—

DEMBI *(Cuts him off, to Adjua)*: Or maybe Stinker?
ADJUA *(To Cranston)*: Adjua. My name. It means born on a Monday.
DEMBI: Adjua's my girl. Every day of the week.

(He plants a kiss on Adjua.)

ADJUA: You hush up, stupid Igbo. *(To Cranston)* This here is my man Dembi.

(Cranston sizes up the situation as he itches his leg, moaning with pleasure as he itches.)

You got worms.
CRANSTON: Worms?
ADJUA: Big ones, ja. Under the skin.
CRANSTON: You a doctor?
ADJUA *(Laughs)*: I mend the sails when the ships come in. Dembi, he mend the rigging. We scrape the casks and make sugar cookies for the market. *(Beat)* Jeffrey, I think you a shred. A tailor. Like me.
DEMBI: He's not like you.
ADJUA: And you work with the cloth for your bread.
CRANSTON: A tailor. Hmm.
ADJUA: Ja, a winter cricket.
CRANSTON: Feed me, please. I'm nithered.
DEMBI *(To Adjua)*: Don't.

(After a moment of consideration, Adjua takes a small piece of biscuit from her pocket and holds it out to Cranston, who snatches it and eats it like he's starving. Then Cranston throws it up again. Adjua and Dembi watch.)

When we pull him out of the water he's wearing fine cloth, well cut. But he's no rich man with worms in his legs.

ADJUA: So . . . maybe he makes one good suit to show off his skill and he wear it every day? Yes. A tailor. A Yankee tailor.

DEMBI: He's sick.

ADJUA: We could fix him up.

DEMBI: He's no use.

ADJUA: Mijn Got, he's a white man. Always got a use. And he owe us his life.

(Dembi thinks this over. Cranston has stopped retching. He fishes out bits of the biscuit from his vomit and eats again. This time it stays down.)

DEMBI: I don't like it. Just me and you, that's what I like.

ADJUA: We fat him up, he can work for us.

DEMBI: Can't trust a man who don't remember.

ADJUA: We can give him all the remembering he needs.

(Cranston collapses, curls up and sleeps.)

DEMBI: And then?

ADJUA: And then he help us.

DEMBI: How? He's got no skills to recall.

ADJUA: We skill him. Then we can sew double the sails. Get double the quid. Oh, Dembi. This thing we pull from the water is a handful of clay and me and you, we're gonna shape it.

Scene Two

PROJECTED TEXT: PASSAGE OF THE WORM:
A FEW DAYS LATER.

Cranston is somewhat recovered but still weak, still without his memory, and at times seems almost amiable. Now and then he lightly itches his leg. He is trying to mend a sail but he's having trouble and pricks his finger. He then puts his work down and begins to scrape one of the empty sugar casks. He licks the sugar from his fingers greedily. His sail-cloth clothes have been modeled to fit him better.

ADJUA *(Offstage)*: Jeffrey! You get your thievin' fingers out my sugar cask.

(Cranston freezes, fingers in his mouth. Adjua appears carrying a cask in her arms.)

CRANSTON: Is it Monday today?

ADJUA: Friday. Don't start.

CRANSTON: You know Monday is the only day I care for.

ADJUA: Dembi hit you again, you keep talkin' to me like this. You mend that sail yet?

CRANSTON: My fingers bleed to prove it.

(Adjua examines his work. She's not happy with it.)

ADJUA: You a poor tailor, Jeffrey. I teach you how to cut the cloth, how to hold a needle, and still your stitching look like lies.

CRANSTON: Why can't I sew if I'm a shred?

ADJUA: 'Cause you a tailor with no skill. A lot of cloth is out there walking on half a stitch 'cause you were so mean you kept the other half. I think that's why you drowned yourself: you were so ashamed of your mending.

(Cranston cries out unexpectedly, in pain, and furiously scratches his left leg. Adjua watches quietly.)

CRANSTON: It's got worse. There! I can see it moving under the skin.

(He follows the itch as it slowly moves around his leg.)

ADJUA: A little bit of worm keep a stupid man honest.

CRANSTON: This is no little bit of worm. I'll cut my leg off, I will.

(Cranston moans in pain.)

ADJUA: Keep quiet or someone will come! Take down your britches.

(Cranston stops itching. He's uncertain as to what Adjua means. She waits and he waits. Cranston hesitates, then drops his sail-cloth trousers. He's got a dirty cloth tied as underwear. Adjua kneels and examines his leg. She's looking for something on his skin.)

CRANSTON: How bad is it?
ADJUA: Shut up, Jeffrey. *(Beat)* Ah. Here's the hole.
CRANSTON: What hole?

(Adjua's eyes are on the wormhole.)

ADJUA: The peephole. Worm has a window in your skin and it peeps out, but if you touch it, it shrink back in. You got to go fishing, ja. That's what you got to do.
CRANSTON: How long is it?
ADJUA: It's still a young one. About a foot long but fat. So fat.

(Cranston groans. Adjua takes a thin pin of wood from her pocket. She's enjoying herself now, though communicating more to the worm than Cranston, and keeping her eye on the worm's movement.)

And it's the fat ones are best 'cause they don't break off easy. We have to catch it peeping out and then wind it about a peg, draw it out slowly, slowly, little by little. Come, come little worm.
CRANSTON: You see the head yet?
ADJUA *(To worm)*: It's a sunny day Friday. Cool breeze out here, not all stink and wet like inside his leg.
CRANSTON: How'd it get in there?
ADJUA: Shhh. There's likely more than one. I try and get the biggest. *(To worm)* Give me your kleine kop. Little face, come to me.

CRANSTON: You think I'm stupid.

ADJUA: Can you remember if you were smart?

CRANSTON: No.

ADJUA: That's my point. There's the head. Don't move. A fat head, too, heel smart one this. I like the smart ones. You may be dumb but your worms, they been reading a book.

(Adjua, in a deft, small movement, rolls the worm a little way onto the peg.)

Got you. Got you. Now I tie the peg to your leg.

(She does so.)

And every day you wind a tiny bit, slowly. Nee be greedy. If you pull too hard or wind too fast you break it. You break the worm it get angry and revenge comes: it bite more and get even fatter. And don't scratch. I seen men scratch 'til the muscle hang out their skin.

CRANSTON: God help me.

ADJUA: A worm does what a worm does. Now we scrape the barrels. You don't work, you don't eat.

(Adjua slaps a scraper in Cranston's hand and they begin to scrape the inside of the barrels. There's hardly any sugar in them, but they find what's in the cracks and put it into Adjua's small, cloth bag.)

CRANSTON: Give us a feel, Adjua.

ADJUA: A feel.

CRANSTON: Of your apple dumpling shop.

ADJUA: Is this you talking or the worm? 'Cause that worm just chew a bit of your flesh then look out his little window. Hello to Dembi. Hello to Adjua. Good morning, Rhode Island. Good morning, city of Bristol. Polite. Your worm got more manners than you.

CRANSTON: It's just I can't remember tuppin' a woman.

(Adjua continues to work.)

ADJUA: Most likely she don't remember it either.

CRANSTON: Nothing in my skull from afore you drag me out of the water, just gruel. Put a stick in it and stir. *(Beat)* What if I'm not a needle man but . . . an astronomer? I love the stars, I do.

ADJUA: No. You a tailor.

CRANSTON: Or I might be a barrister or a gentleman with ruffs.

(Recites, remembering:)

Her lips, her lips are mine
As sure as ball and twine;

(Shrugs) Perhaps I am a poet.

(Recites:)

But I'll cast my plumb and line,
And douse her wound in brine, brine, brine.

(Dembi appears, carrying scavenged goods.)

DEMBI: One thing we do know for sure about you, Jeffrey: you ugly.

CRANSTON: Am I? Am I ugly, Adjua?

DEMBI *(To Adjua)*: There's a sloop half sunk sailed to port. French gunner rammed her, most the cargo washed ashore. I got this. *(To Cranston)* Don't ever think about touching my Adjua. If I look at you tomorrow and see that same idea still floatin' in the wreckage of your skull, I swear I'll—

(As Dembi steps toward Cranston, Adjua throws her arms around Dembi's neck.)

ADJUA: Dembi. What'd you get for the shoes?

DEMBI *(Still watching Cranston)*: Two bits, a damn good bargain! I was sad to see them go, though I think they'll remember my feet. *(To Adjua)* How much we save now? We got to be close. Almost enough, my girl.

CRANSTON: Enough for what?

(Happily, Dembi lifts Adjua up in the air.)

DEMBI: For me and you. And me and you, we're going—

(Adjua covers up Dembi's mouth.)

ADJUA: Bite my hand but shut your mouth.

(He bites her hand.)

Harder. *(She laughs, delighted)* Harder . . . Stop! You'll make me bleed.

(Adjua bites Dembi.)

I got a tasty bite.

DEMBI: Bite me again.

ADJUA: Nee, Lieverd. You wait for the night. There's a couple of spots are missing my teeth. I find them.

DEMBI: Give us a kiss, Monday.

(They have a passionate kiss.)

CRANSTON: You think I don't see it?

DEMBI: Get back to work.

CRANSTON: Aye. I see it. *(To Dembi)* What master is after you, heh? *(To Adjua)* Or you? *(To Dembi)* Slave. That's your name. *(To Adjua)* And yours.

(Adjua and Dembi are momentarily taken aback, though they knew this moment would come.)

Facts are what we got here are two young runaways. Healthy.

(Cranston reaches out and squeezes Adjua's arm, as though testing it. Dembi reacts.)

ADJUA *(Firmly)*: Dembi. Wait.

(Dembi resists attacking Cranston.)

CRANSTON: Strapping. Well shaped.

(Adjua firmly removes Cranston's hand from her arm.)

Oh, what ready rhino I could fill my pockets with. And we're talking gold here, not silver spank. Tell me I lie.

ADJUA *(To Dembi)*: The skunk think he know all about us, love?

DEMBI: 'Course he does. We runaways all the same.

(Dembi says the following like a monotonous story, mocking what Cranston thinks he knows.)

They sail 'em scared, ignorant captives from darkest Africa for Cuba—

CRANSTON: Ha! I knew it.

DEMBI *(Continuing)*: When them sleepy, pitiable slaves finally get to Havana—

ADJUA *(Joining in)*: I'm so sick I can't stand. The captain slap me 'til the skin come off my face but I can't get up no more.

DEMBI *(Continuing)*: Then the white men come on board to feel us if we strong.

ADJUA: Ja. They squeeze our arms.

(Adjua goes to Cranston. She squeezes his arm as he did hers. It doesn't hurt but something about her manner scares him.)

They squeeze hard to find "the defects." To be "carefully avoided."

(Cranston tries to pull away but she hangs on.)

CRANSTON: Get off me.

(Adjua and Dembi simultaneously pick up pieces of chain from the dock and threaten Cranston to be silent. They circle him. Cranston is quieted, passive now. There is something about their manner that makes him afraid to resist. Adjua checks under his eyelids. He submits.)

ADJUA: Film in ye eyes? That's bad.

(Adjua spits on Cranston's arm and cleans the skin.)

Yellow skin. Niet goed.

DEMBI: Means his humors are rotten. Surely means the sickness.

(Dembi slaps open Cranston's shirt.)

Navel sticking out? His stomach's backwards and prone to starve.

(Now Cranston is being inspected and circled by both of them.)

ADJUA: You got bandy legs, ja?

(Nervous, Cranston shakes his head no.)

Then show me. Springe!

DEMBI: Jump, you bastard!

(Cranston shakes his head no.)

Jump or she'll cut you.

(Cranston jumps up and down, once, twice.)

Sharp skins?

ADJUA *(To Dembi)*: It's "sharp shins." Sharp shins.

DEMBI *(To Cranston)*: You got sharp shins, you nigger you?

ADJUA: Open your mouth to speak again—

DEMBI: —and I'll break it. Loss of fingers?

ADJUA: Loss of toes? And his salt?

(Dembi wipes Cranston's neck with his finger and tastes the sweat, like an expert.)

DEMBI: Weak. *(Spits)* No strength left in him. Don't come close to ebony wood.
ADJUA: But his feet, they flat and strong.

(Dembi peeks in Cranston's underwear.)

Dwarfish or gigantic size?
DEMBI *(Laughs)*: Not gigantic, no.

(Adjua is now remembering herself being examined on board the ship. She regards Cranston as though he were a woman captive.)

ADJUA: But look at her ribs. Could scrub your clothes on 'em. And she's got a bandy leg.
DEMBI *(Glancing at Adjua)*: But she's so beautiful.
ADJUA: Nee. She's ugly. Got those long breasts the masters mortally hate.
DEMBI: You can tell by her eyes she's smart.
ADJUA: Lethargic. Idiot. Lunatic. Speak. Speak!

(Dembi slaps Cranston.)

No? Then sing, you Afric bitch.
CRANSTON: I won't.

(In response, Adjua and Dembi, at the same time, smack their chains loudly on the dock. Cranston is subdued.)

DEMBI: I'll knock you down a hundred times 'til you sing.

CRANSTON *(Sings, hesitantly)*: "Her lips, her lips are mine / as sure as ball and—"

(Adjua and Dembi burst out laughing.)

DEMBI: He sings, the bastard!

ADJUA: Ja. He does. Though I never did. The captain sell all the others in Havana but he can't sell me. We sail here to Rhode Island and he try a second time to sell me but no one wants a slave made of sticks. Then there's a ruckus on the docks and I run. My legs so skinny and one of them kort, but when I run my legs don't stop 'til my feet half gone *(Beat)* and then I lay down to die.

DEMBI: And then I find you.

ADJUA *(To Dembi)*: Ja. 'Cause he also running away, Dembi find me.

DEMBI *(To Adjua)*: And Adjua's so light I carry her easy in my arms, for she weigh no more than a little idea.

ADJUA: I raved for days in those arms.

DEMBI: Never could let go of a good idea once it took hold of me.

(Dembi shows Cranston his knife.)

Thinkin' to turn us in? Ha. You take more than ten steps from this dock, I'll cut you from ear to ear.

ADJUA: Dembi will, ja. I seen him do it before.

DEMBI: Now get back to your needle. Work!

(Cranston reluctantly goes back to his work.)

Slave.

ADJUA: Jeffrey. When we get enough coin for the work, we cut you loose.

DEMBI: Sure, we'll cut you loose.

CRANSTON: It's a vessel you're waiting on, isn't it?

ADJUA *(To Cranston)*: You go with Dembi and pick up the other casks when it's dark. Stay off the road.

CRANSTON: Where's this ship headed?

DEMBI: To the center of the world.

CRANSTON: London?

ADJUA: Dembi! Shhhh.

(But Dembi can't resist telling Cranston.)

DEMBI: Africa! Word is there's war in San Domingue and the blackamoors rising. The slaves, they rise up San Domingue! Rise up Grenada! Rise up Jamaica!

(Dembi lets out a celebratory shout.)

ADJUA: Quiet, my love, you bring the officers here.

DEMBI: Whole world's about to capsize, darlin', so you hold on tight to Dembi and he keep you afloat.

CRANSTON: But you were born here.

DEMBI: That's right. Born in Charleston. *(To Adjua)* With the tall trees and my momma's silky breasts swayin' above me. My baby sister and her crazy laugh. But I can't go back to Charleston. *(To Cranston)* You, on the other hand, were born nowhere.

CRANSTON: A nothing from nowhere. A wretch. *(He smacks his head to stress the point)* Well, I'm pierced to the gut with grief. I'm truly pained . . .

(He remembers a tune, so he smacks himself again.)

I think the blows help with rememberin'.

(After another smack, he sings, finding the song as he goes:)

I'm truly pained to be thus stained
And to be neither Abled nor Cained,
But on the other hand
I'll take a proud stand
And proclaim myself well-manned.

(Speaks) Aye. I reckon the tune be finding me.

(Cranston now relishes his song, adding some clumsy footwork. It is as though the song were singing him, rather than he singing the song.)

On land, on land, on land,
I'll roger her holes like the enemy.
The sea, the sea, the sea,
She's the only bitch that ever loved me.

(It seems some of Cranston's memory has returned. Adjua and Dembi stare at him, disturbed.)

I don't see as I'm actually a tailor after all.

(We now notice Balthazar, who has been watching Cranston dance. He steps forward. Cranston, Dembi and Adjua are alarmed and on guard at seeing a stranger appear among them. Dembi draws his knife, stands protectively in front of Adjua.)

BALTHAZAR: Of course you're not a tailor. Foul mouth, foul song. God, I love it. But I'm here for Adjua. That'd be you? And a man named Dembi?

DEMBI: Come no further. What's your business here?

BALTHAZAR: Like squeezing blood from a stone making inquiries among you blackamoors. Makes a man feel like he's got the plague in his face. Well, if it be the two of you, I'm here to let you know that the Captain Liverpool Joe you're waiting on is not worth waiting on: he's drowned.

(Adjua reacts, shocked.)

DEMBI: Drowned?

BALTHAZAR: And the rest of the crew. The ship broke up on the rocks four days west of San Domingue. So to put it plain and simple: your vessel will not come.

DEMBI: Who the hell are you?

ADJUA: Wrecked?

BALTHAZAR: Nothing left of her but a piece of the mast, the squall was that strong. I was near dead when a Portuguese sloop picked me up just off the east tip of Jamaica. Before we went down, I promised Joe I'd find you, and a half dozen others, and I always keep my promise.

ADJUA: Two years we wait for—

DEMBI *(Interrupts)*: Hush. There will be other ships. *(To Balthazar)* What's your name then?

BALTHAZAR: Balthazar. My brethren call me Bal.

CRANSTON: My name is Jeffrey Sinker.

BALTHAZAR: Your name is John Cranston. And you're a sailor. I know this to be a fact, for I took six bits of silver and a piece of gold from a gentleman for the job of your drowning. From the looks of you, I didn't do a very fine job.

(Cranston takes a moment to digest this news. Then:)

CRANSTON: You hog-grubbing blackguard!

(Cranston picks up a piece of wood. Balthazar and Cranston face off.)

DEMBI: Ho! This is our piece of the dock.
CRANSTON: I'll knock out your brains for killing me.
ADJUA: Nee bring us trouble here!
BALTHAZAR: A man with no memory don't frighten me.
DEMBI: You take this off our docks! Not here.

(Cranston swipes at Balthazar but misses. Balthazar holds his ground, warding off Cranston's blows, though Cranston is good with his board.)

CRANSTON: Well the way I reckon it, you should give me half the coins they paid you or they'll find out you didn't kill me and take their silver back.
ADJUA: Who will find out?
CRANSTON: That's what I want know.
DEMBI: Who paid you?
BALTHAZAR: A gentleman. Finely dressed. Don't know his name.

(Cranston swipes at Balthazar again but Balthazar manages to get Cranston into a headlock. Cranston struggles. Balthazar cuts off his air so he can't move.)

But this rat'll not be getting a penny from me. I've a mind to seek out that same man and tell him he needs to kill you a second time, and this time I'll do it for free.
DEMBI: Who's to say you didn't murder your captain, Liverpool Joe, as well?

CRANSTON *(Still in a headlock)*: This gentleman, he paid you six bits and a gold coin to kill me. That's quite a sum. Means I was important. *(To Adjua)* I am important. *(To Balthazar)* Listen to me, you rat fink, English bastard—

(Balthazar throws Cranston down and pulls out his pistol.)

BALTHAZAR *(Calmly, meaning it)*: I'll kill you straight if you say that again.

CRANSTON: Rat fink? Bastard?

BALTHAZAR: Lost my starboard sight when one of them bugs held open my eye and another stuck in the jagged end of a broken stick. Popped like an egg. 'Til this day, when I sleep I feel the splinters that stayed behind pushing to get further in, just like the bloody English. After that, I'm a full-blooded United Irishman!

DEMBI: From the urinal of the planet.

BALTHAZAR: Ay. That's me. "Irishmen of every religious persuasion unite!" "Reform the Parliament!" "Get the English off our backs!" Oh, how we dreamed. And the Americans and French to spur us on with all their fiery visions.

DEMBI: Then what you doing here and not in Ireland to fight?

BALTHAZAR: The English killed so many of us. I was in hiding when I met your Captain Joe in Liverpool. He offered a fairer wage than most.

ADJUA: We never met Joe. It was through the Quakers—

(Adjua takes the book from her pocket. Cranston tries to grab it but misses.)

(To Balthazar) Can you read?

BALTHAZAR: Aye.
CRANSTON: That's my book.
ADJUA: No it's not, schurk. You can't read.

(Balthazar holds out his hand for the book.)

BALTHAZAR: Let me have a look.
CRANSTON: But you found it in my pocket.
BALTHAZAR: The water's blurred it.

(Balthazar reads, with care, warming to it.)

And so he was quiet, and that very night,
As Tom was a-sleeping he had such a sight!

Ah. This be Willie Blake.

(Balthazar looks around, proud of his ability. The others do not respond to the name. Adjua listens closely.)

That thousands of sweepers, Dick, Joe, Ned and
Jack,
Were all of them lock'd up in coffins of black.

(Adjua snatches the book away. She goes to pitch it in the water.)

DEMBI: Adjua. We can sell that!

(Adjua lets out a long string of angry curses in a mix of Dutch and Akan, but doesn't throw the book in the water.)

ADJUA: I hate the koud noise of English: "coffins of black."

Scene Three

PROJECTED TEXT: PASSAGE OF THE TONGUE.

Cranston is examining the peg tied to his leg. He rolls it a tiny bit, slowly. The Shadow watches.

CRANSTON *(To worm)*: Hey little gal, you getting tight on my stick? Gonna miss you when you're gone. Just a wee bit more, darlin'. Oh yes, oh yes . . .

(Cranston tries to roll too much of the worm onto the peg and the worm breaks off.)

Fuck. It broke. The worm broke!

(The Shadow disappears. Adjua enters, carrying mending work.)

ADJUA: She don't fancy you one bit. I told you: nee wind it too fast.

CRANSTON: The bitch, the dirty coquette. Help me peg her again.

ADJUA: You do it. We got to rig this sail, make it hang right.

CRANSTON: Sure. But I'll be straight with you, Adjua: I feel a mighty urge to kiss you.

ADJUA: No, Jeffrey. I say before: no.

CRANSTON: Cranston's my name. Dembi don't need to find out.

(Cranston helps her rig the sail.)

ADJUA: Dembi find out everything. Got a mind like a sky. That big.

(Cranston says the following words quietly, but Adjua recognizes the threat.)

CRANSTON: Don't make me take what I need. 'Cause I will.

(As Cranston regains his memory, a ruthlessness and cunning begins to emerge. Adjua considers her options.)

ADJUA: What kind of kiss?

CRANSTON: Mouth.

ADJUA: Corner of the mouth.

CRANSTON: I can get that for my nutmegs, and more, front end of the docks.

ADJUA: Not without coin.

CRANSTON: I can't kiss without my tongue. *(Beat)* And you'll never sail if I turn you both in. And I will, 'cause I need that reward almost as much as I need that kiss.

(Adjua considers his threat and believes him.)

ADJUA: Schoft. Let me see your tongue.

(Cranston sticks out his tongue. Adjua looks it over. She slowly shakes her head no.)

CRANSTON: What's wrong with it?
ADJUA: I don't want that thing in my mouth. It's alive.

(Cranston snatches at Adjua, but she dodges him.)

CRANSTON: I know how to use it.
ADJUA: Stick it here.

(Adjua makes a fist, then opens it a little so there's a hole.)

We give it a test.

(Cranston is doubtful.)

You think Adjua let you put that stinkin' slab in this mouth that kisses Dembi without testing it first?

(After a moment's hesitation, Cranston grabs Adjua's fist and purposefully sticks his tongue in it. He moves his tongue around. Adjua makes a disgusted noise. Cranston tries out various tongue movements. Then Adjua jerks her fist away.)

CRANSTON: Now look what you done? There's other worms awake with all this fiddling. Keep your kiss then. Give us a hand.

ADJUA: You got your own hand.
CRANSTON: I'll get a fever if I'm left like this.
ADJUA: If Dembi find out he kill you.
CRANSTON: He won't kill a white man.

(Adjua considers.)

I promise I'll be quick. *(Beat)* I won't ask twice.

(Adjua registers this. After a moment, she reluctantly gives Cranston her hand. Cranston examines Adjua's hand a moment.)

Nice hand you got. Clean, too.

(Cranston stuffs Adjua's hand in his pants and begins to masturbate with it.)

Talk to me, Adjua. I know you know got some sweet words . . . !

(As Adjua says the words, without emphasis or break, she does not look at Cranston, but elsewhere, as though reading the words from the air.)

ADJUA: Land cloth crop field sugar rice—
CRANSTON: Jabber on something sweet!
ADJUA: Virginia Carolinas Georgia trade price—
CRANSTON: Talk dirty to me!
ADJUA: Blacksmith tobacco carpenter cook runaway—
CRANSTON: Aye, I remember this feeling.
ADJUA: Slave member children sails—
CRANSTON: Squeeze, yeah. Squeeze.

ADJUA: Atlantic West Indies sister machine—
CRANSTON: Damn it. You ain't helpin' me here!

(Cranston has lost his desire. Adjua pulls her hand away. Silence for some moments.)

Adjua. I got to have your mutton.

(Adjua shakes her head no. As she backs away, she spits at his feet.)

ADJUA: Nooit. Never!

(Suddenly, Cranston grabs Adjua's throat with one hand, tightly. It happens so fast that Adjua cannot react.)

CRANSTON: Aye . . . I will have you. Or I'll sink you both.

(Cranston drags Adjua away.)

Scene Four

PROJECTED TEXT: PASSAGE OF YEARNING: MORE DAYS LATER.

Another area of the docks. Dembi and Adjua are alone and taking a rare break. Dembi sips from a small bottle of whiskey and sings a couple of lines from an old song from Charleston. Adjua is studying her book.

DEMBI: You know what makes the best sound in the world?

ADJUA: Ja. A merchant vessel, near shore, breakin' up in a storm.

DEMBI: No.

ADJUA: The sails of a vessel we call our own—

DEMBI: Nope. You do.

ADJUA: Me? How?

DEMBI: When we're under the cloth and you're making those little moans—

ADJUA: —that sound like the devil clearin' his throat—

DEMBI: That's when I know I'm still alive!

ADJUA: You're corned. Give that back to me. We got to sell that whiskey—

DEMBI: Ah, be sweet to me, Adjua. Here.

(Adjua gives in and shares a sip with Dembi.)

You got something you want to tell me?

(Adjua is silent a moment.)

ADJUA: Dembi. I think the time is right to make our child . . .

DEMBI: Who you thinkin' about, woman?

ADJUA: No one. But we can find a good man to help us.

DEMBI: We find the man when we've got the right earth under our feet: Africa. That's where we'll make our family. And our child'll flip this world quick, turn it inside out.

ADJUA: We got to get another vessel to sail or my heart break.

DEMBI: We find some more Quakers and we make a new plan.

ADJUA *(Grabbing his face)*: Please don't make me wait too long.

DEMBI: I promise.

ADJUA: Then I believe you.

(Adjua releases him. Dembi says the following like "facts.")

DEMBI: Woman. You're a stone in here. Your weight gives me an ache in my gut: there's no room in me but for you.

ADJUA: The whiskey sure make my Dembi sweet.

DEMBI *(A warning)*: Without your weight I'd come loose from these docks, float up high over this stinkin' city 'til Dembi is gone.

(Adjua kisses him on the forehead. He doesn't respond.)

ADJUA: Come. We got to get back to work.
DEMBI: You go. I won't be far behind.

(Adjua goes. Dembi looks out over the waters, unsettled.)

Scene Five

PROJECTED TEXT: PASSAGE OF THE GIBBET.

Adjua is writing purposefully in her book and singing an African lullaby. Cranston is asleep at a distance, curled up. Dembi paces back and forth, clearly agitated. Suddenly Balthazar enters dragging an old gibbeting cage behind him. At the bottom of the cage are the remains of the last incarcerated man.

BALTHAZAR: Now this be a catch! And let the almighty law in all its mistaken righteousness fret about the whereabouts of poor Jonah here and his iron whale.

ADJUA: That cage belongs to the courts!

DEMBI: Are you mad? Hide it. Quick!

ADJUA: No one saw you take it?

BALTHAZAR: No.

DEMBI: No one followed you?

BALTHAZAR: Cut him down last night. Least I could do considering I sort of recognize his . . . smell.

(Balthazar studies the human remains in the now upright cage. Dembi grabs the cage as if to get rid of it. Balthazar holds onto it.)

DEMBI: If we're discovered with this—

BALTHAZAR *(To cage)*: Ah, brother. It's no way to end one's stay on earth. Though you did have a good view of the sea when you drew the last card. Damn to hell those who lorded it over you.

ADJUA *(Touching the cage)*: We get some good coin for this metal.

DEMBI: Maybe he's no brother. Maybe he's the tar who beat Adjua on the water.

(Dembi stabs at the remains in the cage.)

BALTHAZAR: No, leave him be. One day he's sitting in a wee church with his family. Without a coin, but clean. And then he be dragged out, slapped on a ship, and two days later he's chin down in the sea, face gone to a cannonball. Still in his Sunday suit.

DEMBI: How'd he get in the cage then? Maybe his lust for the gold of black flesh.

BALTHAZAR: Or a coal miner, black lungs all his life! West Riding way. Shipped out a hollow, terrified scrap of a man.

DEMBI: Maybe he held a whip and my brothers felt it.

BALTHAZAR: Maybe this be James, who struck a midshipman for beatin' a fellow tar and was pitched overboard for his trouble. Shark meat. I sailed with all of them.

Just spare parts. And each brute, penniless, scared and mean. My brethren.

DEMBI: Our brethren. I say, Death to the masters!

BALTHAZAR: For they know what they do!

ADJUA: But now, Lieverd. Please can we hide the cage?

(Balthazar throws a tarp over the cage, just as Cranston suddenly wakes saying Adjua's name.)

CRANSTON: Adjua. *(Beat)* My heads a-burstin'.

DEMBI: That's the last time you say my woman's name. Swine. Our vessel is not coming, no; so we don't need you anymore. You can go.

CRANSTON: Go where?

DEMBI: I don't care. Just git.

BALTHAZAR: There's one mean bastard out past these docks thinks this tar's dead. If he stays here, he's safe.

DEMBI: Exactly. *(To Cranston)* Go.

BALTHAZAR: And that same bastard might think I cheated him and then come after me, so if you don't mind, I'll stay on just a few more days myself.

DEMBI *(To Balthazar)*: As long as you work.

BALTHAZAR: Aye.

DEMBI *(To Cranston)*: Be gone or I'll gut you.

CRANSTON: You can't just turn me out!

DEMBI: You heard me.

(Dembi and Adjua now turn away to a task. Cranston, his head still hurting, hits himself in the head a couple more times and then bursts out with remembering.)

CRANSTON: All I knows in pieces. Like a ship that's been rammed— *(He breaks off)* But there's this one craft, way off, keeps moving through my skull. I think she be a slaver. A two-masted vessel. I think her name be *(Beat)* the *Polly*.

(Adjua is stunned.)

ADJUA *(Whispers)*: The *Polly*?
DEMBI *(To Adjua)*: No. He's lying.
CRANSTON: That's the vessel that sails in my head.
DEMBI *(To Adjua)*: Adjua, he's trying to play us.

(Cranston becomes afraid of their reaction.)

ADJUA: What. What was the captain's name?

(Cranston can't remember, or he won't remember.)

CRANSTON: I don't remember.

(Adjua nears him. Dembi takes out his knife.)

DEMBI: Get off my docks now or I'll flay you.
ADJUA: What was his name?

(Cranston shakes his head. It seems Dembi will cut him.)

CRANSTON: You said if I helped you find another vessel, I could sail with you.
DEMBI: There is no vessel! And if there were, we'd never sail with a tar who's boarded a slaver. You're lucky we let you live.

(Dembi shoves Cranston away.)

CRANSTON: It were the crimps who got me.

(Cranston moves to go. Adjua calls out to him, to keep him from leaving.)

ADJUA: Jeffrey.

CRANSTON: They'd pay off my landlady, whiskey me up, and I wake on board when a seagull flies over and shits in my drunk open mouth.

ADJUA: Jeffrey.

CRANSTON *(Angry)*: It's John Cranston!

ADJUA *(Evenly)*: Tell me the captain's name.

CRANSTON: I said I don't recall.

DEMBI: Leave it be, Adjua.

(Dembi tries to pull Adjua away.)

ADJUA: De Wolfe, ja. Ja?

(Cranston slowly turns around. He recognizes the name. Dembi steps forward.)

DEMBI: De Wolfe? That was the name of your captain?

CRANSTON *(Quietly)*: Yes.

(Adjua begins to keen. It's as though a terrible pain has flooded her body. Even Dembi is reluctant to touch her. Cranston is afraid.)

DEMBI *(Gently)*: Adjua, hush. Hush up. Someone will come.

(Adjua stops abruptly. She clutches at Dembi.)

ADJUA: Get the short sail I been mending. Now!

(Dembi does as she asks.)

Spread it out on deck.

(Dembi spreads the sail out quickly. Adjua turns to Cranston and suddenly pulls out a knife. She motions to the sail.)

Lie down on it.

(Cranston shakes his head no. Dembi punches him in the gut. Then Dembi and Adjua wrestle Cranston onto the spread-out sail. Balthazar watches but keeps a distance.)

CRANSTON: Ne'er once took a slave ship of my own will! I was crimped on board four slavers.

(Dembi and Adjua deftly roll Cranston up in the sail until he can no longer move; all that is showing are his feet and head. As Cranston and Balthazar talk, Dembi and Adjua expertly wrap rope around Cranston to keep him tight inside the sail.)

BALTHAZAR: Four slave voyages and you lived? You've a hearty bone in you. Most tars are dead after two.

(Adjua and Dembi now pull Cranston upright, so he's standing on his own feet, with only his head showing from the cylinder of sail cloth.)

CRANSTON: I ne'er killed a captive.

BALTHAZAR: But you beat them.

CRANSTON: Everyone was beaten. Including me.

BALTHAZAR: Should've joined the United Irishmen.

CRANSTON: I'm not fuckin' Irish! You going to torture me now?

ADJUA: Nee. We're going to drown you. Do it right this time.

BALTHAZAR: I won't have any part of murder.

CRANSTON: You hypocrite. I was good enough for you to kill the first time, weren't I?

BALTHAZAR: I best be headed on now. *(To Adjua and Dembi)* Pity we couldn't find another vessel. I wish you both luck.

DEMBI *(To Cranston)*: You touch my Adjua?

ADJUA: Dembi. Throw him in the water—

DEMBI: You hush up, woman. *(To Cranston)* You touch her?

ADJUA *(To Cranston)*: Klootzak.

CRANSTON: Not me, no.

ADJUA: Hoerezoon.

DEMBI *(To Cranston)*: Walk to the edge, slaver. Walk to the edge and jump.

(Cranston edges to the water of his own accord. He readies himself to jump.)

BALTHAZAR: Do you need a push?

CRANSTON: No. Thank you. I believe I can manage.

BALTHAZAR: Good-bye, ye ole tar. Tough luck got him in the end, John Cranston.

(Cranston leans to jump just as Liverpool Joe appears. He's been watching them. Joe is finely dressed.)

JOE: Cranston? John Cranston?

CRANSTON: Aye?

JOE: Who testified in Newport just eight weeks ago against one son-of-a-bitch captain for the murder of a slave?

CRANSTON: I did?

JOE: Let me shake your hand. You're a hero, you are.

(Cranston turns to Joe but they can't shake hands. Joe ruffles Cranston's hair instead. Adjua and Dembi are wary. Balthazar now comes forward.)

BALTHAZAR: You're a ghost, man. Liverpool Joe were drowned in the squall.

JOE: That I was, Bal. I dropped into the deep but I didn't want for air. A school of blue fish, each fish tiny as a fingernail, swam into my mouth and down into my lungs and gave me oxygen.

BALTHAZAR: Come here, you ugly mermaid. Let me look at you.

(Balthazar and Joe hug heartily. Adjua and Dembi are stunned by Joe's appearance and the revival of their dream of escape.)

ADJUA: And you be the Liverpool Joe who will take us back home?

JOE: That's me. Captain Liverpool Joe.

(Dembi touches Joe's clothes.)

DEMBI: You sure are dressed nice for a sailor.

(Joe smacks his hand away.)

JOE: Though the squall took every piece of something from my ship, I kept my best coins in the skin pockets of my foot.

DEMBI: Skin pockets?

(They all look at Joe's feet, which are wearing fancy shoes.)

BALTHAZAR: Always keep the banks under your heel.

JOE: When the turtlemen who rescued me hit the coast, I had nothing but a piece of string 'round my waist. I bought these from a gentleman. Well. He was dead and wouldn't hear of me paying him. We parted fast friends.

CRANSTON: Captain Joe.

(Cranston tries to come near Joe but falls down and rolls along the dock.)

Were you with me aboard the *Polly*?

JOE: I was not. But they sure are talking sweet about you up and down the coast. I'm glad to see the rumors of your death were hasty.

CRANSTON: So I once thought myself. Your friend here tried to murder me for silver.

JOE: Did he? *(To Balthazar)* Now that's a surprise, you old lunkhead, you.

BALTHAZAR: Pay a poor man to kill a poor man and something stinks, but aye, Balthazar took the coin.

(Joe has an idea.)

JOE: How much did they pay? Are they still paying?

(Joe winks at Balthazar.)

CRANSTON: Hey!

DEMBI: We got the coin for passage, sure, but how will we get a vessel?

JOE: My dear sir, you are speaking to The Liverpool Joe. Raised in the city of that same name by a duchess. I can ride a horse, fence and even do a spot of acting, when called for.

BALTHAZAR: All at the same time, heh Joe?

(Joe ignores Balthazar.)

JOE: I'm a capable man and a worthy captain. *(Bowing)* Your worthy captain.

BALTHAZAR *(Teasing)*: Where's your stage now, Blackie? Where's your pretty horse?

JOE *(Ignoring Balthazar)*: And I have commandeered another ship.

BALTHAZAR *(Surprised)*: You're still lying?!

JOE: I swear on the most delicate toe of my long-lost but once-beloved duchess.

BALTHAZAR *(To Dembi and Adjua)*: When he swears on the delicate toe, that's when I wager you can believe him.

ADJUA: We've a vessel to sail, Dembi. Our dream come awake again!

DEMBI: If you play with us, I'll kill you.

JOE: Calm, man. Calm. We leave for Africa, via London and Portugal to avoid the hard currents, in three days' time.

DEMBI: And the other passengers?

JOE: We've lost track of the other four, so we'll pick up some replacements further on. For now, it'll be just the two of you.

(Adjua runs to Joe and takes his face in her hands.)

ADJUA: Thank you, dear sir. Heel bedankt.

(Joe smiles, enjoying the gratitude. Dembi menaces him.)

DEMBI: Why you so eager to help us? I don't trust you.

ADJUA: Dembi!

JOE: "If a man have not love in his heart for his fellow creatures, all his other virtues are not worth a straw." Quobna Ottobah Cugoano. Otherwise known as John Stuart. Black abolitionist and brilliant man of letters. Resides in London—

BALTHAZAR *(Teasing)*: And be sure Joe knows him well.

JOE: Did a spot of revising his book for him: *Thoughts and Sentiments on the Evil and Wicked Traffic of the Commerce of the Human Species*. Improved on it, if I may say so—

DEMBI: Enough talk. Let's get to work to reverse this "wicked traffic."

JOE: Of course. Cranston! I'll need you to help me sail her.

DEMBI: He's not coming with us.

ADJUA: Nooit!

JOE: But he's rumored to be one of the ablest tars this side of the water. We must have him.

CRANSTON: Thank you, no. This ole sea crab's had enough of water. I'm headed inland.

JOE: Look. Sooner or later the ones who want you dead will find you again. Not so lucky next time. You board with us and you'll be safe. We'll hire more crew up the coast.

(Cranston knows Joe is right.)

CRANSTON: So they're talking about me in Newport? I'm famous then?

JOE: Your name certainly is: John Cranston. Still, as I heard it, the name was often followed in the taverns with, "Captains unite and cut his throat," "Hang the dirty traitor," and "He'll ruin the trade for the rest of us." I knew then you were a decent man.

(For the first time, Joe considers that Cranston is rolled up in a sail.)

Though I cannot say the same about your taste in dress.

Scene Six

PROJECTED TEXT: PASSAGE OF THE SPINDLE SHANKS.

A few days later. Dembi, Cranston, Joe and Balthazar prepare for their voyage in various stages of excitement. On the docks are demijohns of water, casks of salt beef, salted cod, beans, biscuits, gunpowder. Balthazar sharpens cutlasses. Dembi oils pistols. Joe reads some charts as he speaks. Cranston mends a rope.

JOE: It's unheard of! Unheard of to refuse your captain. It's said you sailed from Newport that May and on to the coast of Africa, to Annamaboe, from there to Accra where the vessel got the chief part of her slaves, and from thence to the West Indies. Then a slave was taken sick, which you took to be the pox . . . Go on.

CRANSTON: Can't remember it clear.

JOE: Don't be a muckworm, cough it up—

CRANSTON: You're so damn keen on the story, you tell it.

JOE: But we want to hear it from you! *(To the others)* They say that for Cranston's day in court, the Quakers dressed him up like a gentleman, gave him a book to flash at the judge so he'd presume him a tar of culture.

DEMBI: But he can't read.

JOE: The judge didn't know that!

BALTHAZAR: Was the slave woman or man?

JOE: A woman.

DEMBI *(To Cranston)*: What was her name?

JOE: Why try and stop your captain from throwing her overboard? That was mutiny, man.

CRANSTON *(Angry)*: Damn you. Let it rest! It's behind us now.

(All are quieted some moments by Cranston's angry outburst. Joe buries himself in his charts again. Balthazar nicks himself on a cutlass.)

BALTHAZAR: These cutlasses got more rust on them than iron.

CRANSTON: Gunpowder's damp.

DEMBI: I'll wager these won't fire nothing but air.

(Joe looks up from his charts.)

JOE: I never say no to a bargain.

BALTHAZAR: A bargain? He should have paid you to cart this shite away.

DEMBI: Why won't you show us the vessel?

JOE: She will show herself when she's properly dressed. I've got a man on her at this very moment.

BALTHAZAR: And this man, I'm sure, is drunk.

JOE: He has assured me that he can stand, despite the barrel fever, for long periods at a time, and wield a hammer and nail.

BALTHAZAR: I paid for half these provisions. Don't you forget it.

JOE: The money you spent you got from Cranston's drowning, so don't grouse.

BALTHAZAR: If I had my choice, I'd commandeer a mighty navy ship, with eight hundred crew to sail her. And I'd go up and down the coast, plundering and warring any nation's vessel I come across. I'd be the terror of the ocean. I'd be wanted on three continents. I'd be the famed United Irishman Pirate. And all of you would tremble at my name.

JOE: We tremble now, Bal, for fear of you tangling yourself in the shrouds and pitching yourself overboard. *(Beat)* Though he can steer.

BALTHAZAR: I should be captain. You drove us into that squall, near killed the both of us and surely the others drowned. It's my turn.

JOE: Balthazar. You're my first mate.

DEMBI: Must we have a captain?

CRANSTON: Aye, we must. I won't sail without one. When things get bad—

JOE: And they will.

CRANSTON: When we're sick with the flux—

JOE: And we will be.

CRANSTON: When we hit a storm and we're sinking—

JOE: Two or three times at the least.

CRANSTON: When one of us crew tries to desert at port in London, most likely me—

JOE: I'll have to use the pistols.

BALTHAZAR: I was thinking I'd jump ship in Lisbon—

CRANSTON: We'll need a captain to keep our manners about us—

JOE: —to see our corpses through to the end, even if it's down to the bottom of the ocean where we'll say to one another a polite "adieu." Any more questions?

BALTHAZAR: That's one blackamoor who don't speak like a slave.

JOE: Ah. But I was born on a slave ship, and as an infant given to Lady Stretmore of Liverpool.

BALTHAZAR: Rumored to have the finest spindle shanks in the city!

JOE: She wore me on her arm like a jewel.

DEMBI: You were a dog, then?

JOE: Oh yes. But a jewel of a dog, a priceless pet. I wore a collar with diamonds encrusted 'round. Noli me tangere. White servants bathed me. Though I admit they pinched me when they could and called me a mungo, a little black bastard. And then one night—

BALTHAZAR: Here comes the shipwreck.

JOE: —the duke tore me from her innocent arms. You see, once little black boys become young black men they are no longer trusted with the ladies. Our collars are too tight and they fear we will break them.

DEMBI: How many voyages you make so far, carrying poor souls back to Africa?

JOE: I've made two voyages. This will be my third.

DEMBI: What happened with the other two?

BALTHAZAR: Don't ask him.

JOE: May they rest in peace. There is nothing more difficult than reversing the Atlantic passage. But third time is lucky, I'm sure.

CRANSTON: And Joe here didn't have John Cranston on board then. And remember, even if I can't, that I'm the best.

JOE: You people have no idea what ingenuity it takes to buy or steal a ship when you're a sable captain. The vessel waiting for us now, her name was *Friendship*. I have given her a new name.

CRANSTON: It's bad luck to change a vessel's name.

JOE: But general bad luck is always specific good luck for Liverpool Joe. Her new name is: the *Leak*. I have acquired papers on her, and good forgeries they are too.

DEMBI: The *Leak*?

BALTHAZAR: What the hell name is that?

CRANSTON: The *Leak*?

BALTHAZAR: God help us.

JOE: No one will hanker after our ship with such a name. Her name is her protection. And the bitch will aspire to prove me wrong in naming her such. I've promised her if she carries us safe to Afric I'll rename her "*Never*." *(Beat)* "*A Leak*."

CRANSTON: How's the hull on this ship?

JOE: She's got two cannon. Will come in handy if we're attacked.

BALTHAZAR: And her hull?

JOE: I admit there are a few holes where one can see the most curious kinds of fish swimming below her . . . But once we set sail, Cranston will keep her afloat, being half carpenter himself.

CRANSTON: I am?

DEMBI: I don't care if we sail on two boards with a sack for a sail. We're ready. And if we all drown, Mami Wata will pick our bones 'til we clean as coral and carry us home.

JOE *(To Dembi)*: You're a tough young buck. Brave. Thirsty for adventure?

DEMBI: I never been to sea, Captain.

JOE: Ah. *(Beat)* Then you will be my cook. Can you cook?

(Dembi nods yes. Joe sensually touches Dembi's cheek.)

Curacao, San Domingue, Tortola. The blackamoors rising. And this new bastard world will be ours, friend. They can kill and enslave us one by one, but together we are indestructible as a people. And our cause is just, for "the destroyers and enslavers of men cannot be Christians, for Christianity is the system of love." Cugoano again. Though that's actually my line; the scum bucket stole it from me. There's one man in San Domingue who is so powerfully strong he can lift a boat, and his mind's so wide he can suck up the ocean, swill its currents in one breath, and spit it out again! Toussaint L'Ouverture.

BALTHAZAR: I bet this Toussaint plays the harp like you, eh Joe?

JOE: Toussaint has a lieutenant named Dessalines. *(To Dembi)* They say Dessalines is so beauteous that the enemy is momentarily stunned when they encounter him. Perhaps you are his distant cousin, for you are quite handsome, too.

DEMBI: Adjua's my woman. I'm handsome for her.

JOE: On a ship, the line between woman and man becomes . . . Well. A wee bit blurred, and when a tar is lonely any sweet hole that's warm and moist will—

CRANSTON: Lay off him, Joe. A captain should keep a little distance.

JOE: So he should.

(Joe trails his finger across Dembi's mouth and down to his neckline as he speaks.)

What's your story, Dessalines? There's a hint of conundrum about you . . . I've a wee hunch you were gentled by your master. Well cared for? A sparse handful of us were, though we're ashamed to admit it, coddled. Honey-gummed.

BALTHAZAR: A word-pecker, our Captain Joe.

DEMBI *(To Joe)*: My mother was his slave: Master Samuel. On Tuesdays he'd give me a biscuit. Thursdays a wedge of apple. Saturdays he tied me to his bedpost and flogged me. For years the same thing.

(Joe stops caressing Dembi's neck.)

Biscuit. Apple. Then the flogging. Coddled? He didn't swive me like he did the others, men and women both, but he liked to make me wail with the pain of the flogging. There was a sound he liked especially. So I learned it well. Some days he didn't need the whip 'cause I'd start to wail before he could lash me. Honey-gummed, huh? Want to know how it sounded? That squall that he was looking for, that moan the masters are living for?

(Dembi begins a strange, sorrowful sound, but Joe gently puts his hand over Dembi's mouth and silences him. Joe nods to Dembi, in acknowledgment that he was wrong.)

JOE: All right men. Listen up! I am your captain. Balthazar here, my first mate. Cranston my quartermaster, boatswain and carpenter. Dembi, our cook. We're a crew now and I will respect you if you respect my vessel. I will protect you with my life. If you bring trouble to my ship, I will tie a cannonball to your neck and pitch you overboard without breaking my stride.

Scene Seven

PROJECTED TEXT: PASSAGE OF THE *POLLY*.

Most of the provisions have been packed and taken away. Only a couple of crates remain. Adjua is packing gunpowder into a pistol. Cranston appears.

CRANSTON: You got to oil the inside of the barrel or it will stick.

ADJUA: We should've let you drown.

(Cranston is silent. Adjua busies herself with cleaning the gun.)

The slave that got sick on your vessel, the *Polly*. *(Beat)* That was my sister. We were together on your ship.

(Adjua oils the inside of the gun.)

CRANSTON: I don't recall your face.

ADJUA: Why would you? I was nix to look at. But my sister, men remember her.

CRANSTON: I didn't kill your sister.

ADJUA: I was in the hold down below. I couldn't see. How can I know? *(Beat)* Tell me how she died.

(After a few moments, Cranston begins to speak. The following exchange has slight echoes of a court hearing.)

CRANSTON: There were one hundred forty-two Coromantee on board the *Polly*. One hundred twenty-one delivered alive.

(Adjua calmly points the pistol at Cranston's crotch. Cranston just looks at her. He knows she'll use it.)

ADJUA: About my sister.

CRANSTON: The captain, he tied her to the maintop, to keep her away from the rest. Because she was sick. It was the pox.

ADJUA: Had she any victuals while in the maintop?

CRANSTON: Yes.

ADJUA: Was she alive when she was let down?

CRANSTON: Yes.

ADJUA: How do you know she was alive?

CRANSTON: Because I seen her alive about two minutes before in the maintop.

ADJUA: Then what did the captain do?

CRANSTON: After two days, when the watch was called at four o'clock, the captain called us all aft and says he, "If we keep the slave here, she will give it to the rest and I shall lose the biggest part of my slaves." Then he asked us if we were willing to heave her overboard. We made answer "no." We were not willing to do any such thing. Upon that he himself run up the shrouds, saying she must go overboard and shall go overboard—ordering one tar, Gorton, to go up with him—who went. They lowered her down from the maintop.

ADJUA: Who launched her overboard?

CRANSTON: They lashed her in a chair the captain brought from his cabin. There was a tackle hooked upon the slings 'round the chair.

ADJUA: Did you not hear her speak or nee make any noise when she was thrown over?

CRANSTON: No. A mask was tied 'round her mouth and eyes that she could not, and it was done to prevent her making any noise, that the other slaves might not hear, lest they should rise against us. They lowered her down the larboard side of the vessel.

(Adjua lowers the gun, then takes hold of Cranston's face to look him closely in the eye, to see if he is telling the truth. Dembi enters in the background, sees this, mistakes it for intimacy, and exits.)

I said those very words in court. Aye.

(Adjua lets go of Cranston's face and spits.)

Your sister was very beautiful.

ADJUA *(Cuts him off)*: Don't speak of her again.

(Adjua begins to leave.)

CRANSTON: After the captain threw her overboard, he said he was sorry he had lost so good a chair.

(Adjua just looks at Cranston, then away, her pain and anger so great, but she will not show it to him.)

What was your sister's name?
ADJUA: That I will never tell you.

(Adjua leaves.)

Scene Eight

PROJECTED TEXT: PASSAGE TO SAIL.

A few hours before they sail. Restlessness, excitement. The men do some last minute preparations. Joe is still wrestling with the charts. He shows their route to Dembi. Cranston and Balthazar keep playfully snatching the charts away. Then Balthazar reveals some whiskey. They all cheer. Balthazar passes it on as each man makes a toast, though Balthazar drinks none for himself.

BALTHAZAR: Ready to sail, men?
JOE: Ready to sail?
ALL: Aye!
JOE: Ready to die?
ALL: Aye!
JOE: The currents are strong!
CRANSTON: Provisions packed tight!

BALTHAZAR: Then a toast to the *Leak*.
CRANSTON: May she hold her breath in the squall.
JOE: May her captain prove both fierce and true!
ALL: Aye!
JOE: Where'd you get the whiskey, Bal?
BALTHAZAR: A kindly gentleman at the tavern.
CRANSTON: What gentleman?
BALTHAZAR: I didn't pay. He gave it for our voyage.
CRANSTON: Gentlemen don't give sailors whiskey for naught.
JOE: Balthazar. Did you tell him our plans?
BALTHAZAR: Goddamn you, I'm no fool.

(Joe and Cranston are not convinced.)

But I swore to him that one day I'd sail a real ship, a vengeful ship, not some laughable leaky schooner. Sure he asked our route. But no. I told him it were secret. He said he was a Quaker.

JOE: Quakers don't go to the taverns.
BALTHAZAR: The Wet Quakers do. Relax, mate. I took the whiskey for you, Joe; I don't even drink the shite myself!

(Balthazar holds out the whiskey to Joe, who relents and drinks. They all laugh, drink, relax and make small talk. Adjua enters and joins in the gaiety. She makes marks in her book and shows them to Balthazar and he nods approval. Then Adjua makes a toast. The men cheer.)

ADJUA *(To Dembi)*: It's happening. *(To all)* Finally it's happening.
Smile, my love. Are you not happy?

(Adjua embraces Dembi, but he moves away from her. Now Dembi makes a toast.)

DEMBI: A toast. A toast to our voyage!

(They all cheer.)

And I take this liberty now to tell you all, friends, that I'll not be sailing with you.

(Silence. Dembi drinks to his own toast. Adjua believes it's a joke. She laughs.)

ADJUA: Dembi, he so excited he plays the clown. Lieverd, you are my clown.

(The others now laugh as well, but it's forced.)

DEMBI: I'm staying on in Bristol.
ADJUA: You're coming with us.
BALTHAZAR: We need you on deck, mate.
JOE: And you've paid me a fine sum to carry you, which I'll not refund.
DEMBI *(To Joe)*: You can keep the spank, Captain. These dock I sweat and grind on, are mine. This is my home.
ADJUA: Dembi.
DEMBI *(To Adjua)*: Woman, we made a lively place here, with naught but planks and water—
BALTHAZAR: Oi. It's his first time to sea. The lad's got cold feet. *(To Dembi)* Not to worry. Balthazar will be at your side.
CRANSTON: And so will I. The vessel needs you.

DEMBI: Beach horner. Worm's hole. You don't need me for anything. And I won't stoop so low as to sail with slaving muck like you. Never. *(To Adjua)* Monday. You gave me my name: Dembi. That is not my name. Take the name back with you to Africa. My name is Morgan. *(To all)* I wish you all safe passage. I stay here.

(Adjua just stares at Dembi. She knows he is serious but she doesn't know what to do to change his mind. Dembi gathers up a few things to leave. Silence as the others watch him. Finally, Adjua speaks.)

ADJUA: I say it again, your true name, your Afric name: Dembi. Not Morgan. Because we plan this for years. Because we are finally ready to sail. *(Beat)* Because I am carrying our child.

(Dembi freezes. He can't believe what he's hearing.)

DEMBI: What you say?

ADJUA: I'm carrying our child. I nee want to tell you 'til we are safe on the boat. Adjua say to you: our child, Dembi.

(Dembi is stunned.)

Lieverd. This is what we dreamed for.

DEMBI: Our child?

(Adjua throws her arms around Dembi's neck.)

ADJUA: Ja, our rising, our revolt. Our miracle that'll clear the path we couldn't—

DEMBI: Our miracle? Adjua, my girl. Adjua, my Monday . . .
CRANSTON: Carrying a child is poor luck for a vessel.

(Suddenly Dembi roars and attacks Cranston, as though to kill him. Joe and Balthazar pull him off. Dembi tries again, fiercely, to get near Cranston, but he's blocked by the other men.)

BALTHAZAR: Ho! Settle down.
JOE: Come on, man. The child will be a talisman for our journey.
BALTHAZAR: That's right. We'll make do.

(Joe and Balthazar settle Dembi down.)

JOE: Let me be the first to congratulate you both.

(Joe raises the bottle to toast, but the others are silent, concerned with Adjua's condition. Adjua notices this.)

ADJUA: Men. Listen to me: I'm strong. I promise you, no matter how heavy I get with child, I be useful on board. I be fit and able. This is our sign to sail, ja. For all of us to sail!
BALTHAZAR: Come on, men: a cheer for the new wee passenger coming aboard the *Leak*!

(All cheer again, this time with more conviction. The men shake Dembi's hand and slap him on the back, though he is still in a daze. Cranston is still wary.)

Joe. Here's your chance if there ever was one. But no horses, no violins and no fuckin' Garrick.

JOE: You're a wretch, mate. I'll never sing for you again.

(Joe turns away from Balthazar as though hurt, but then suddenly jumps up onto a keg and sings, with a beautiful and well-trained voice:)

I served a kind old duchess
Placed my head on her ample chest
She so pale, me so black
And the duke's heart going tickety-tack.
Learned to read, to write, to sing,
Even to play the violin,
Warmed by fire, warmed by silk,
And the duke's head going tackety-tick.
Shipped away on the sly,
Fell down from the palace into a sty,
Cargoes of men, white and black,
Dance to the whip, tickety-tack.

(Cranston, Joe and Balthazar join in the song together, and chase one another around the docks in celebration. Then the sailors all dance together, and it's an impressive jig.)

ALL:

Shipped away on the sly,
Fell down from the palace into a sty,
Cargoes of men, white and black,
Dance to the whip, tickety-tack.

(Amid the celebrations, Adjua takes Dembi in her arms. After some moments, he responds and returns the embrace. The celebrations continue, with harmony

seemingly restored. But then Adjua silently sinks to her knees. At first it seems she is simply taking a rest, and the others do not notice, nor do we, but then blood spills between her fingers where she clutches herself. One by one the men stop cavorting, in shock. Only now do we see that Dembi is holding a knife.)

ADJUA *(To Dembi)*: Oh my love. You have killed us.

(Before anyone can react, we hear the shrill scream of police whistles and running feet. All are startled.)

JOE: God curse your stupid tongue, Balthazar; we're discovered! *(To Balthazar and Cranston)* Take the woman up. Quick. Run. Run! To the vessel and ready her sail!

(Cranston and Balthazar each take the now almost-unconscious Adjua by the arm and carry/drag her between them. They exit in a panic. Joe snatches up the scattered charts and whatever evidence has been left behind. He stands for a moment, looking at Dembi, who has not moved, still staring at the knife. Their eyes meet.)

(Evenly) Run, man. Run.

(The voices are closing in. Now Joe runs. Dembi stands alone on the docks. He won't run. We now hear the voices of various constables.)

CONSTABLES' VOICES *(Offstage)*: There's one of 'em. Fire if he moves. Find the rest of them!

(Dembi turns his head to look after the way his friends left. Dembi still does not move, waiting for whatever horror will overtake him. We hear one last, long, loud scream of a whistle as the lights go black.)

Act Two

Scene One

Projected Text: Book Two. Passage of Lady Bristol: Forty-Six Years Later.

The Shadow enters, sprinkling powder like a path for Bristol to follow.

Bristol, Rhode Island. Dawn. 1837. The seediest tavern on the docks. Sparse. Small. Run down. The owner is Cranston, now in his seventies. He takes pride in the place. He is behind a rustic bar. His body is worn out but still reluctantly strong. Bristol appears. She has just arrived from England after a tough journey, but she is full of restrained energy. She has a lady's veneer but also the confidence of the assassin. Below the surface, something more tough, passionate and bawdy emerges.

BRISTOL: I'm looking for a scoundrel.

CRANSTON: I don't serve liquor to women. Any women. *(Beat)* What kind of scoundrel?

BRISTOL: The top-drawer kind.

CRANSTON: We only got the cheap sort here.

BRISTOL: I'm looking to meet a senator.

CRANSTON: That's too fine a scoundrel to drink under this roof. So you're looking for work in a white man's home?

BRISTOL: In a manner of speaking, yes.

(Cranston cleans the bar with a dirty rag.)

CRANSTON: Well, there's not many who's hiring. When his heart went "pop," the merchant's bank president, and he 'scaped to the pine box, the whole city got sick with the speculative fever. And now there's been runs on the rest of the banks. Anyone who's got a half penny has snatched it back as the giants fall. 'Course most of us have nothing to snatch back but the crabs from our crotch as they bid us "adieu." Public faith breakin' like sticks, snap. Even the ships aren't moving. Hard to believe these waters once floated the finest privateers that built this Yankee nation. Plummeting, crushing of rebellions, even our pricks no longer rise. I thank the devil that a man still needs a drink.

BRISTOL: I need. Access.

CRANSTON: Don't all us poor bastards.

BRISTOL: I need a referral.

(Cranston feels a slight pain in his thigh.)

CRANSTON: Shhhhh. No need to wake, my gal.

(Bristol looks around, confused.)

Don't start again, ye ole bitch.

(Bristol thinks he's referring to her.)

BRISTOL: Sir, there's no call to be—

CRANSTON: Shhhhh. Go back to sleep now, my darlin'. Don't be pesterin' me. Cunny tooth!

(Cranston suppresses a sudden cry of pain.)

BRISTOL: I . . . I've come to—

CRANSTON: That's enough!

(He takes a shot of whiskey, then finishes cleaning up some glasses that he spits in, then dries with the dirty rag.)

Deliverin' liquor to more'n a dozen fine houses besides running the tavern. Need to finish up here. Open again at noon. Get out now, Misses. All this damn jabberin' and she's come awake.

BRISTOL: I'll wait with the other men out back.

CRANSTON: Those aren't men. They're puddles of shit and whiskey, not stirred. They won't wake 'til nightfall.

BRISTOL: I've heard it said you were a sailor.

(Cranston ignores her.)

I have coins.

CRANSTON: If that be true, I could take 'em right now. No one to stop me.

BRISTOL *(Warning him)*: I've sailed from England in a stinking vessel packed too full. The biscuits were so thick with vermin, they walked of their own accord.

CRANSTON: My last boatswain? The hogs on board sucked his heels to the bone.

BRISTOL: The eyelids of the dying were eaten by rats.

CRANSTON: The first officer had me prop him up with two barrels and make him steer. Feeney died standing up, still sailing the proper course.

BRISTOL: Two weeks into the voyage, a lady gave birth to half a child. Both of them were thrown overboard.

CRANSTON: I've cut an abscess the size of your fist from my own gut and sewed it back up myself, without blackin' out.

BRISTOL: I worked as a servant, like a slave, saved, for more than twenty years. I bought my freedom.

CRANSTON: I dined with the great blue-spotted shark, the Greedy Robber.

BRISTOL: Then I opened a grocers in the rookeries of London.

CRANSTON: Teeth as long as my arm. I lost four fingers.

BRISTOL: I sold dried biscuits, sweets and, in season, apples and pears. I've never married, though I've given birth. Twice. Both died of the fever before age three. I dug their graves with my own hands.

(It seems Bristol has won the "contest.")

CRANSTON *(Sings)*:

Long and strong, you swim and curl.
That's my darlin', that's my girl.

BRISTOL: I have papers to prove I am free.

CRANSTON *(Sings)*:

If I could, I'd snatch your head
And cut you to pieces 'fore you were dead.

(Cranston tries to snatch the papers from Bristol's hands but she's too quick.)

Those papers would fetch a nice sum on the market.

BRISTOL: Your songs are unpleasant. Have you no wife?

CRANSTON: No, I thank God. My mother once told me she loved me, but it smacked of revenge. The most faithful gal in my life? Well. *(Grimaces with pain)* She's a Guinea worm. Picked 'er up when I was a lad off the Bight of Benin.

BRISTOL: Proof you are a sailor.

CRANSTON: I'm a barman now for thirty years.

BRISTOL: You're not easy to find. John Cranston. I know your name.

CRANSTON: And you live to tell the mighty tale. Go prosper.

BRISTOL: I need an introduction to the Linden Place.

(Cranston makes a noise of disbelief.)

CRANSTON *(Quietly)*: Do you really think the senator would be inclined to allow a black bitch, just off the boat, who's not been half pretty for many a year now, into his stately home?

(Bristol is undaunted by his insults.)

BRISTOL: My name is Bristol Waters. May I trust you?

CRANSTON: Certainly not.

BRISTOL: You are likely a man of substance, Mr. Cranston. You testified against your captain, James De Wolfe, about the murder of a slave on board your ship. You were a young man then. It has even been said that you were handsome.

(Cranston scoffs and busies himself.)

Even in London they still speak of the trial. We had our abolitionists too.

CRANSTON: I weren't an abolitionist.

BRISTOL: In Salem, there's a new antislavery society, run by sable women. Oh yes. And another one here in this city. And elsewhere.

CRANSTON: That kind of revolutionary talk in Bristol, *(Beat)* Bristol, leads to a wry mouth and a pissen pair of breeches.

BRISTOL: I need your help. John.

CRANSTON: If, and that's no promise, I could get a word to Senator De Wolfe, what would I say?

BRISTOL: That an educated woman has come from London to pay him a call.

CRANSTON: Should I mention the small factual that you're a blackamoor?

BRISTOL: That an educated free black woman has come all the way from London . . .

CRANSTON: . . . to engage him in the most respectable of conversations?

BRISTOL: No. *(Beat)* To kill him.

(Cranston takes this in for some moments.)

CRANSTON: I'll suggest tea and cakes be served when you arrive.

(Now Cranston casually puts a pistol on the bar, but he doesn't look at Bristol.)

Why?

BRISTOL: Specifically? The ocean. He strapped a living being, my aunt, into a chair and threaded her hand over hand into the dark.

CRANSTON: Take care to whom you tell your business, woman. Other people's business is profit if it gets out.

(Cranston and Bristol regard one another.)

You got a good knife?

(Bristol slowly reveals a knife. Cranston whistles, impressed.)

A hunting knife. And fine.

BRISTOL: I brought it from London. Honed the blade myself.

CRANSTON: During the War of 1812, the senator was king of the privateers—

BRISTOL: Yes, and seized dozens of enemy ships. I once heard it said that he can buy the ground out from under you so quick you'll have no place to stand without trespass. *(Beat)* You testified against him. He must despise you.

CRANSTON: I don't matter to him now. Go back to England. Live.

BRISTOL: I've no money for the return passage.

(Bristol sways; she's dizzy.)

CRANSTON: When'd you last eat?

BRISTOL: I'd like a drink.

(Cranston waits. Bristol searches, then finds a last coin in her dress.)

CRANSTON: I don't serve no wibble; I got fair whiskey.

(Bristol grunts "no" to most of his suggestions.)

Irish, scotch, rye. And no piss in it. Kentucky bourbon. Bub. Or taplash, if you can keep it down. *(Mocking)* Something soft, Ma-dei-ra?

BRISTOL: Jamaican rum?

CRANSTON: Kill Devil? I only serve Kill Devil to men big as boats cause it'll knock a hole in your stern.

BRISTOL: Give it to me.

(Reluctantly, Cranston serves the Kill Devil to her. She drinks it in one big gulp. She shudders deeply and represses a scream. Cranston, now competing with her, takes a shot himself, and does his best to hide the burn better than she has. Then Bristol pushes her glass forward again.)

Just a finger more. *(He serves it; she downs her Kill Devil)* You knew my uncles: Balthazar and Liverpool Joe.

(Cranston feels the worm bite on hearing the names, but the pain passes.)

You jumped ship, Mr. Cranston, just after I was born. For years we stayed on the water. My uncles moved people and supplies around the islands, ferried slaves to freedom. Cursed and hunted by both slavers and navy men, Joe and Balthazar were wanted on three continents. What men they were.

CRANSTON: Aye. I've heard the stories.

BRISTOL: When I was five years old, a gang of blackbirders met our ship in port. Do you know what a blackbirder is, Mr. Cranston? The lowest form of carrion. They re-enslave the free and sell them back to slavers. I was bought by a West Indian sugar planter on his way home to a big estate. Then sold on at seven to a captain headed for London, who gave me to a gentleman.

CRANSTON: Captain Joe and Balthazar. It's said they were drawn and quartered.

BRISTOL: Yes, they were.

(Cranston suddenly cries out as the worm attacks his leg.)

CRANSTON *(To worm)*: Damn you, leave me be.

BRISTOL: You knew my mother, Adjua. What do you remember about her?

CRANSTON: I've no use for memory. A black spot on a potato, I cut it out.

BRISTOL: She wasn't the kind of woman a man could forget—

CRANSTON: I'm closing up now. Christ. She's not been biting me like this for years. Fuck!

(The worm stops biting him. He rests.)

BRISTOL: What happened to you after you left our ship?

CRANSTON: Nothing ever happened to me again.

BRISTOL: You knew my father: Dembi Morgan.

CRANSTON: So! It's that rotten bastard, is it, who's sent you?! If he thinks he—

BRISTOL: My father was hanged shortly after they caught him.

(Cranston realizes his mistake.)

CRANSTON: Get out of my tavern and don't come back.
BRISTOL: My father is alive?

(Bristol stares Cranston down. Cranston is the first to look away.)

Is it the same Dembi we speak of?
CRANSTON: Dembi Morgan was the refuse and dregs of the docks, and that when he was still young. I haven't seen the man in many a year. But if you're looking to use that knife of yours, it's him you should be using it on.

(Bristol doesn't understand.)

BRISTOL: Is my father alive?
CRANSTON: You heard me.
BRISTOL: Tell me where he is!

(Cranston shakes his head and turns away: he'll tell her no more.)

Tell me!

Scene Two

Projected Text: Passage of Too Damn Much to Drink.

Bristol, still somewhat tipsy and disoriented from the Kill Devil, wanders the docks, lost. We see figures crisscross the stage, busy with the day. We hear the haunting groan of ships, sails rubbing against their ropes in the harbor, perhaps the coughing of a sick man in the distance, and bits of muffled music from a tavern a good ways off. At moments, Bristol thinks she sees someone walking ahead of her who looks like Adjua, but then the figure disappears. Then more clearly, we hear a sound that at first might seem like rats, but it's something else: something swinging in the breeze.

BRISTOL: Hello? Is someone there? Hello? Might you help me?

(Exhausted, Bristol sits. She feels Adjua kiss her forehead while The Shadow watches. Suddenly, out of the dark, a life-size cage appears, slightly larger than the one seen in Act One. It is swinging to and fro from a beam on the docks. A dead man has been gibbeted in the cage. Bristol is terrified and covers her mouth, almost retching from the smell. The man's clothes are rotting and so is the body underneath. There is a small pile of something unthinkable under the cage that has fallen off the decomposing body. But Bristol cannot help her curiosity. She inspects the dead man from a distance.)

I've seen you somewhere before? But no. No. *(She moves closer in)* Maybe. Do you remember? Was it London, outside the Cocoa Tree in Pall Mall? You were, you were . . . It was raining and you were just leaving and your mouth was still stained with chocolate . . .

(She sits near the corpse and sings to herself.)

> Drinking chocolate at the Cocoa Tree,
> Oh how happy one can be.

I'm sure we exchanged a few words. You looked, well, more lively, of course. But even then I said to myself, he is not long for this world. He drinks in a hurry and chocolate is not good for one's morals. *(Beat)* But I don't know you, do I? You're just a slab of worm beef caught in God's locket and there's no key.

(She remembers a line of verse and recites it as a prayer for the body:)

And by came an Angel who had a bright key,
And he open'd the coffins and set them all free;
Then down a green plain leaping, laughing, they
run,
And wash in a river and shine in the sun . . .

(Bristol freezes when she hears a voice.)

BODY: Damn it. There goes another toe. The pieces keep dropping off.

(The body in the cage perks up a bit. It recites:)

And so Tom awoke; and we rose in the dark,
And got with our bags and our brushes to work.
Tho' the morning was cold, Tom was happy and
warm.

BRISTOL AND BODY:
So if all do their duty, they need not fear harm.

(Bristol inches forward again. She doesn't believe what she is hearing, and yet she converses.)

BRISTOL: I've never taken to that last line.
BODY: Irony, my lamb. It's ironic.
BRISTOL: I've had two drams of Kill Devil; I almost never drink.
BODY: Oh, for a dram of Kill Devil to wash the tickling maggots from my throat. My brain is thick with flies. Abuzz.

(The body follows the trail of a fly with its eyes. Bristol does too.)

BRISTOL: Do I know you?

BODY: My name is William. You've got my book in your hand. Though sadly only the verse, and those intrusive scratchings between my lines . . . Have you seen the engravings?

BRISTOL: Yes. At the bookshop.

BLAKE: I miss the painting far more than the words. The right colors can give you a blow to your chest, a deadly blow, much like love. Words are merely what come after love, to placate the emptiness. *(Beat)* I never was happy with that last line either. Irony is a cheap ejaculation. I prefer its whorish neighbors: polemic, expostulation, mockery, hyperbole, provocation, abuse, which polite society so often misreads in my verse. I'll change that line. What would you prefer I say?

BRISTOL: William Blake died in England twenty years ago. I cannot be speaking to him.

BLAKE: Why not? I conversed with my dead brother Robert all my life.

BRISTOL: In a gibbeting cage?

BLAKE: No. In my head. But it's a similar machine.

BRISTOL: I'm lost. You frighten me. And you have a terrible smell.

BLAKE: I won't apologize as this isn't my body. It's rare that I land in a rotter like this. Not pleasant at all. But when someone, in this instance you, recites my verse near the dying, for a brief few moments I'm here again, inside their expiring flesh. Dying or dead is the only harbor I can reach now. That's my deal with the Almighty for having penned him a few rather fine verse in my time. I first saw God's face when I was with fever and only four years old.

BRISTOL: The Almighty?

BLAKE: He stuck his head through my window and I screamed and screamed 'til his colossal hand brushed my cheek and I grew calm in the ice of his touch. He visited again when I was a youth. I lay steaming with contagion in my bed—dying, of course, this time for love. God came into my tiny room and filled it near to bursting. His quiver of sound, light and jubilation, well, it made me quite giddy. He slipped a giant finger inside my nightdress and touched my hard and frenzied flesh until I poured out of myself and into his gaping oblivion. He left me empty as a sack; I never felt such peace again in all my life.

BRISTOL: Shame on you for such blasphemous preaching!

BLAKE: I never told a soul while I lived. But do you really believe that Jesus never had his cock sucked? The Son of God? Ha. The body is a wee coffin of black whose key is in the pocket of our Lord and the world inside him with it. *(Beat)* Now what do you want, woman? I have only a brief time in the bodies I visit. Then back to my nothing I go.

BRISTOL: I am looking for my father.

BLAKE: Aren't we all? I thought you were looking for a senator.

BRISTOL: Well, yes, that too, but my father's name is Dembi Morgan.

BLAKE: And tell me, my dear, what makes this father your father?

BRISTOL: I am his flesh and blood.

BLAKE: Metaphorically speaking?

BRISTOL: I don't understand.

BLAKE: Of course you don't. But you do wish to find him?

BRISTOL: Yes. No. *(Beat)* I've had a picture of him in my head all my life. He's a prince. He's beautiful. What would you say if you came upon a daughter you'd never known?

BLAKE: My Jesus. Another one. And a black one, too. But, as "all men are alike, though infinitely various," come into my arms.

(Bristol involuntarily steps toward the cage as though to be embraced.)

Stop. Not these arms! They cannot hold you.

BRISTOL: That's what they all say, said, the bastards. My lovers. Mostly sailors. The same rotten tune: "We cannot hold you, we cannot pleasure you, we cannot love you. Because you're not really here." And they were right in a way. I was always trying to get *(Beat)* here. And my "here" with them was always a "there" and they knew it. Does that make sense?

BLAKE: Not in the slightest.

BRISTOL: No matter. My scamps are all at the bottom of the sea with Neptune or Poseidon. Tick, tock went the clock, click, click went their bones. I held vigil while they held saltwater.

BLAKE: A lonely occupation.

BRISTOL: "Love seeketh not itself to please."

BLAKE: "So sung a little Clod of Clay." But surely there was one who loved you true?

BRISTOL: Kilter Atlas.

BLAKE: Exquisite?

BRISTOL: Oh yes. You had to look at him aslant or hurt your eyes. But the tighter I held him—

BLAKE: —the quicker he slipped away? So sung a little Clod of Clay.

BRISTOL: You already said that.

BLAKE: I'm a poet, repetition dogs me.

BRISTOL: My father is alive and I . . . I want him to stay a prince in my mind.

BLAKE: Perhaps he is. Or perhaps this very meat in this cage is your father. How can one ever truly know? Still, you are your father's daughter, so I will tell you where he resides.

BRISTOL: But how could you know that?

BLAKE *(Shrugs)*: How could I know the life of a chimney sweep when I've never been up a chimney?

(Bristol considers this.)

There are seven miles of dock on this coast.

(Bristol despairs.)

BRISTOL: Oh . . .

BLAKE: The little pinkie has fallen off. I can feel it missing. Put it in your pocket: it will point your way. The only ones still hung and gibbeted on these docks are rebels, so it's a rebel's bone. Go on. Pick the finger up.

(Bristol hesitates, then gingerly picks up what she thinks is the pinkie.)

No. That's the winky.

(Bristol drops it.)

I pray he used it well.

(Bristol sees the finger and picks it up.)

You'll feel when you're close by its tremble.

(The body is now still. Blake's spirit is gone, as though it had never been there. Then Bristol goes.)

Scene Three

PROJECTED TEXT: PASSAGE OF FATHERS.

The far end of the docks. This part of the docks, over forty years later, is now even more neglected; the boards are rotten. The place seems only a memory of itself. Dembi is an old man now. He is tending two used-up sailors, Nesbitt and Gifford. One black, one white, respectively. The men are dying, and yet they retain a stubborn energy. Dembi uses a rag to squeeze water into their mouths and scrapes a paste from a piece of wood with a stick and feeds the men. First Gifford, then Nesbitt. As the three of them talk, the dying sailors lick and gum the stick, hungry. Dembi treats the dying men harshly, but behind this is a gruff tenderness.

NESBITT: Your porridge is like liquid gold. How you make it so sweet?

DEMBI: A squirt of morning urine and it's honeyed just fine.

GIFFORD: Liar.

NESBITT: If I knew dying'd be so pleasant, I'd have started years ago.

DEMBI: You been dying too long as it is, you scowbanker. When I took you in I figure you dead in three days. You gave me two coins. They're long used up. Your dying is past three weeks now. I should take your shoes as credit.

NESBITT: Not yet. Please.

GIFFORD: I'm not overdue. I said from the start that this old wharfinger would take ten days to die, and today just starts the eighth.

DEMBI *(Still feeding them)*: In all the long years I take you bastards in for a pittance, not one of you ever die on time. You linger. You linger some more. Lingering is 'bout the only thing left you know how to do. I should leave you crawl in a salt barrel to die.

GIFFORD, NESBITT AND DEMBI: I'm quitting after you're gone.

GIFFORD: So the song goes!

DEMBI: You Dutch ones die quick, but you Portuguese, you sing too much. Germans, they grind their gums. The Yankee, he suck his thumb to the bone with fright. The French? Well. They the French. But they all come to Dembi to die. Last month I had a tar crawl all the way from Boston on his one knee 'cause a shark took his other.

NESBITT: But Dembi don't come free.

GIFFORD: Nope. Dembi finger our last silver. You should buy a suit. Rags is all you are.

NESBITT: It's not respectable to the dying.

DEMBI: I save my coin.

NESBITT: For what, old man? You'll be dead soon, too.

GIFFORD: And then who will bury you?

DEMBI: Who needs their arse wiped?

GIFFORD: Not me. Can't shit no more.

NESBITT: I need a wipe. Still got the flux.

(To pester Dembi, Nesbitt and Gifford sing "The Maggot Song." Dembi ignores them. He gets a bucket and cloth.)

Open my heart, have a good look inside
That's where all the maggots thrived.
They came on board when I was a youth
They devoured my soul and my sweet, cunny
tooth.

(Dembi expertly wipes Nesbitt clean.)

DEMBI *(To Nesbitt)*: I'll make you up some salve for those blisters. Take the sting out.

GIFFORD AND NESBITT:
Oh why did I love her? It rot me away,
'Til my knees were my feet and with elbows I'd
pray.
I long for the days before that first bliss
Before song turned to wailing and rum into piss.

(Gifford suddenly begins a terrible, hacking cough.)

DEMBI *(To himself)*: Whoever say death come quick is a liar. Death never quick.

(It seems that Gifford has stopped breathing.)

NESBITT: He gone?

DEMBI: Shhh.

NESBITT: Yep. He gone.

(Gifford does seem dead. Then, suddenly, his eyes snap open.)

GIFFORD: Still here!

(Dembi is relieved, but he pretends otherwise. Bristol appears and watches them.)

DEMBI: Well, don't brag about it. All right. You two ready for the day, so you better commence with your dying. I got four lined up waitin' for Dembi's care. If I could still do six at a time . . .

GIFFORD, NESBITT AND DEMBI: —but my back only let me do two.

(Bristol steps forward. She's overwhelmed at seeing Dembi. At first she can't speak.)

BRISTOL: Dembi?

DEMBI: Damn! What you doing here now? It's daylight. You're supposed to be here Thursday, child. Hide. Hide! Quick, under this sail.

(Bristol is so startled that she lets Dembi push her under a pile of sail and cover her up. The two sailors look on warily.)

Now don't you move from there. Not a sound. I'll take you to the others when it's dark. Who sent you here without letting me know? Idiots. Crazy. All of us be hanged.

GIFFORD: She's no dying sailor.

NESBITT: She's no sailor.

DEMBI: You two hush up. *(To Bristol)* You need water?

BRISTOL: Yes, please. I'm dreadfully thirsty.

GIFFORD AND NESBITT: Dreadfully?

(Dembi hands some water to Bristol, under the sail.)

BRISTOL: Thank you. You're very kind.

DEMBI: You got coin?

BRISTOL: Not anymore.

DEMBI: I'll give you some bits to hold you over. Where you been hid?

BRISTOL: We docked last night.

(Dembi wonders at this British accent.)

DEMBI: You come by boat?

BRISTOL: Yes.

DEMBI: Who hid you? First names only.

BRISTOL: I paid for my own passage from London.

(Dembi considers this. The sailors also raise their eyebrows. Dembi now flips back the sail. Bristol peeks out. She can't take her eyes off Dembi.)

DEMBI: You're no runaway slave.

BRISTOL: No, I'm sorry.

DEMBI: Who are you?

BRISTOL: Bristol Waters. A free woman.

DEMBI: Then why you ask for Dembi?

BRISTOL *(Hesitant)*: I was . . . I was so small when I was born that I fit in the palm of my uncle's hand. His hands were rough from working the sails and they chaffed my skin.

GIFFORD AND NESBITT: Chaffed?

DEMBI: Look. If you've no business here with Dembi, you move on.

(Bristol tells the story as though it's her own personal myth, as though the story is telling her. She tells it without drama, and yet she knows she is speaking in a kind of code, and she is hopeful that Dembi will recognize the story.)

BRISTOL: My mother was dying on the deck of our vessel when we sailed. She had a hole in her breast three fingers wide, and when the sun hit the crack of the wound, the crew could see the corner of her heart. They were afraid to see her living when she should be dead. But then a fish leapt on the starboard side of the vessel and landed on deck. The crew had never seen a fish so red before, as though filled up with blood, and my uncle, he snatched the fish and squeezed it over my mother's mouth and its liquid poured into her and gave her blood. Then he used the tiniest bones of this same fish, boiled clean, to suture shut her wound. And taking turns the crew chewed their beef to porridge and fed her like a bird would feed its chick. *(More pointedly to Dembi)* And she didn't die. She never woke again but she did not die. *(Beat)* We sailed for England short of crew, but we made the crossing. We provisioned our vessel at different ports. Three days out Lisbon, my mother's waters broke. Or something broke, for it poured fast out of her and my uncle couldn't stop it. As I was born, my mother died.

(Bristol pulls up her sleeve to show Dembi, who feigns disinterest.)

This is where my uncle, Liverpool Joe they called him, nicked me with his knife when he cut me from my mother's womb.

(Dembi freezes when he hears Joe's name.)

Balthazar, he nursed me on biscuits and gruel, and I did not die, though as a child I was so thin, he said, that when I stood to his side, sometimes he couldn't see me. I never knew my mother. Her name was—

DEMBI AND BRISTOL: Adjua.

BRISTOL: My uncles said you were hanged. But you're alive.

DEMBI: Who says I'm alive?

BRISTOL: I am your flesh and blood.

(Gifford and Nesbitt look at one another and grin. Dembi is stunned.)

NESBITT: You old scoundrel. You said you'd no family.

GIFFORD: The old man's got a fine set of whirligigs on him after all!

BRISTOL: I am your daughter.

DEMBI: Hush up, woman. I have no daughter.

BRISTOL: I am your child. Cranston said—

DEMBI: John Cranston?

BRISTOL: Yes. I met him at the tavern.

DEMBI: I should've killed that bastard forty years ago.

BRISTOL: My Uncle Joe told me the constable ran my mother through with a sword, but you, you fought them—

DEMBI: Is that what they told you?

BRISTOL: Balthazar said you were a hero.

DEMBI: You're out of your mind!

BRISTOL: You made it possible for the rest to escape. You sacrificed yourself for us—

DEMBI: Shut up, woman. "Your uncles" deceived you. Stupid, gullible . . .

(Dembi suddenly grabs Bristol by her throat, menacingly.)

Ignorant wench.

(Dembi lets Bristol go. Bristol recovers.)

BRISTOL: Cranston says you're refuse. He said I should use a knife on you. Why? *(Beat)* Well I don't care. Do you know how many times I've dreamt—

DEMBI: It weren't the constable and watch that ran your mother through. I did.

BRISTOL: What. Are you saying?

DEMBI: I killed your mother.

BRISTOL: I don't believe you.

DEMBI: Go. There's nothing here for you.

BRISTOL: It's not possible . . .

DEMBI: It's the truth.

BRISTOL: Absolutely not. *(Beat)* Listen to me, Father . . .

(Dembi now unbuttons his shirt and opens it. We see that Dembi has breasts. Bristol is stunned.)

DEMBI *(Firmly)*: I am not your father.

NESBITT: Am I dead or does our old man have dugs?

GIFFORD: Our old man is an old woman.

(Dembi covers up again.)

BRISTOL *(Quietly)*: No. It can't be. *(Shouts)* No!

(Bristol is stunned. She runs.)

Scene Four

Bristol has been running wildly along the docks, trying to escape what she knows. She collapses into the fetal position and holds herself tight. Bristol has a vision/nightmare: As she lies there, water begins to rise up until it touches the docks, then further, 'til it covers the docks, then further, 'til it begins to cover Bristol. She is able to scream once.

BRISTOL: No!

(Dark Shapes, that we thought were a part of the docks, rise up—inhuman shapes. The Shadow appears just as a chair descends on chains from the air. The Dark Shapes put The Shadow into the chair. The Dark Shapes bind her wrists and ankles to the chair. Now Bristol dreams of her aunt's drowning.

At first, her aunt is raised up in the chair, over the dock. Bristol herself feels the terror of drowning, while The Shadow is completely motionless throughout, showing no emotion.

Then The Shadow/Bristol's aunt is lowered down into the water. Bristol relives her aunt's terror and death, struggling hard to breathe, struggling against invisible ropes.

We hear the wild sounds of the ocean. When Bristol's aunt is high up, swinging in the chair, the rope is cut and the chair falls into the ocean. Bristol screams as the chair plunges into the ocean. Everything goes black.)

Scene Five

PROJECTED TEXT: PASSAGE OF OLD BONES.

Dembi has appeared at the tavern. Dembi and Cranston have not seen one another for many years. They are on guard. Two old men with sharp knives.

DEMBI: Jesus, you got ugly.
CRANSTON: I was always ugly. What do you want?
DEMBI: You sent her to me.
CRANSTON: The hell I did.
DEMBI: I didn't know the child lived. But you knew.
CRANSTON: Aye, and she's fine, ain't she?
DEMBI: If Adjua had told me what you'd done, I'd've stuck that knife in you.
CRANSTON: Yep. She was faithful.
DEMBI: We'd of found a good man to give us a child, someone grand like Liverpool Joe.

CRANSTON: Your name was the only word she spoke across the Atlantic.

DEMBI: You're lying.

CRANSTON *(Explodes)*: To God I wish I were! *(Quietly)* You killed her, and she still loved you.

(Dembi takes this in. After some moments, Dembi leaves.)

Act Three

Scene One

Projected Text: Book Three.
The Passage of Names.

The De Wolfe mansion, Linden Place. De Wolfe's elegant study. A huge window overlooks the harbor. A beautiful, imposing chair. De Wolfe's back is to us. He stands gazing at a painting: Nicolas Poussin's The Arcadian Shepherds, *which seems to take up the entire back wall. He is an old man, impeccably dressed. While there is frailty, there is also an obstinacy and vigor about him, a solidity and purpose. After some moments, we hear a servant lead Bristol into De Wolfe's study. Bristol stands watching De Wolfe's back for some moments.*

DE WOLFE: *Et in Arcadia Ego.*

(A pause.)

BRISTOL: "I too am in Arcadia." *(Beat)* I've seen the original at the Louvre.

(De Wolfe still does not turn around.)

DE WOLFE: Paris has a copy. This is the original. On quiet loan for as long as I wish. Flawless. I could stare at it for hours. *Et in Arcadia Ego*. Even in Arcadia there is death. *(Beat)* The absolute clarity. The balance. The harmony of all its parts working as one aesthetic machine. Are not these the elements to shape a man?

(Bristol does not respond. De Wolfe shifts his gaze slightly, looks out the window.)

I can see the waters from this window. It always creates in me a yearning for voyage. John Cranston came by to warn me of your visit, though I had the sense it was less about protecting me than you. He still bears a grudge for having himself unsuccessfully drowned. I don't know if this grudge is because I wanted him dead or because I failed at the task.

(Beat) Welcome. I've been waiting for you for over forty years. Or someone like you. You're almost old. I expected a younger—

BRISTOL: It's taken me a long time to get here.

DE WOLFE: May I assume that you've already visited the brewers, bakers, draymen, masons, caulkers, glaziers, blockmakers, riggers, joiners, ropewalkers? Not to mention the butchers, blacksmiths, coopers, shipwrights, painters, carvers in the city? It certainly must have been a long day for you. For we were in it together. I financed eighty-eight voyages, transported—

BRISTOL: Enslaved—

DE WOLFE: —more than ten thousand Africans. I still own three of the finest plantations in Cuba. I've made all that's formed you.

(Bristol is silent. De Wolfe looks at her a moment, then back out the window.)

You're here about the chair. *(Beat)* One stupid slip of the tongue and I've already been consigned to the dark end of this country's short history. Yes, I did say I regretted the loss of my chair when she went overboard—

BRISTOL: —when you threw her overboard.

DE WOLFE: More than a few good chairs went overboard in those decades.

BRISTOL: She was my family.

DE WOLFE: It's over. Slaving is illegal now.

BRISTOL: But not slavery.

DE WOLFE: Mr. Cranston says you have a knife.

BRISTOL: And I know how to use it.

(De Wolfe wonders if he has underestimated her.)

Et in Arcadia Ego. (Beat) Vigorous. Sunburnt. Hair thickened with the salt of the waves. Excellent at reading the winds. That's how I imagined you as a young man.

DE WOLFE: I was as absolute in my small dominion as any potentate on earth. I crafted legislation.

BRISTOL: Striding up and down the deck, thundering your orders with the grace and purpose of a Greek God. Not an old man shrinking in his silks and laces.

DE WOLFE: She was carrying the pox. If it had spread, I'd have lost the rest. As it were, I only lost twenty-one.

BRISTOL *(Calmly)*: Butcher.

DE WOLFE: I was responsible for her death, yes. But let's come at it from another angle. Allow us to negotiate: I have been further educated since then, and it's only in retrospect that I can say I would not do the same today. But that day your aunt was classified as cargo. I threw cargo overboard.

BRISTOL: My mother grieved for her sister all her short life. *(More to herself than De Wolfe)* Grief. An affliction so formidable it can take generations to—

DE WOLFE: You speak splendidly. You've evidently received a first-class education. Have you considered the fact that you'd not have such refinements had you been born wriggling in the mud on the Bight of Benin?

BRISTOL *(Steady)*: Executioner. Assassin. Cutthroat.

DE WOLFE: Why look at things with such a pestiferous air? Within this delicately nurtured wrath of yours, might you be able to conceive of the notion that I am now truly regretful?

BRISTOL: If there is a hell, and I have come to believe from the continuous hints and murmurs in this world that there is, I pray you are already in it.

DE WOLFE: And yet I enjoy my pipe. I reread the classics and I am enriched. I admit I've made mistakes, but does that mean I cannot enjoy, deeply enjoy, the sight of a fork-tailed flycatcher eating peanuts from a string I've hung in the garden?

(After a moment:)

BRISTOL: Ever since I was five years old and my uncles told me her story, I've been with my aunt, in my sleep, underwater, tied to that same chair, sinking in the dark.

Have you ever tried to breathe underwater? The trick is not to resist the water pushing to get in. Once your lungs fill, you relax, and that's when you gather up to pull free from the bonds. And sometimes, on a good night, we rise to the surface. What is inside you?

(Bristol looks at the painting.)

A model of classical principles of composition? Harmony, in all its parts?

DE WOLFE: So deliciously smug in your condemnation of me, aren't you? You may return to . . .

BRISTOL: London.

DE WOLFE: Ah, I thought as much by your accent. You may go back to that damp city, leaving me to burn in my perdition. But are you sure? *(Beat)* I've lived in your mind for decades. You've always been here, always will be here, with me. Am I wrong? Why, the thought of me is so familiar I'm like family to you now. And why not? The facts are that it was I, Captain James De Wolfe, who was at your aunt's side the last minutes before she drowned.

(Bristol listens, still.)

As I tied the mask around her eyes, I felt her breath on my hands. Her mouth was hot with fever when I stuffed in the rag to keep her quiet. Her bare arm touched mine as I worked to secure the ropes. Our breathing came as one as I began to lower her, hand over hand toward the water. *(Beat)* You understand, what I am saying is—in those last moments, I possessed her entirely.

(Suddenly, with a shout, Bristol expertly flips De Wolfe onto his back. She straddles him and takes out her knife.)

BRISTOL: Not entirely, no. To you, Captain, my aunt was merely one of the ten thousand of the millions whose name you never knew. But she had a name.

DE WOLFE: All right. I'd like to know her name. I understand. How much do you want for it? Let's see, I'll give you— I warn you, I'm a shrewd one with exchange.

(Bristol releases De Wolfe and sits in his chair.)

BRISTOL: I don't think I've ever encountered a man as *(Beat)* uninhabited within as you are. What I'm looking at now is not a former senator, privateer and slaving captain but a lonely old sack of skin—putrid with self-pity and entitlement. You're not large enough to be my tyrant.

(Bristol exits.)

DE WOLFE: Wait. Come back here! How dare you! As a young man, I was the toast of this city! Even men found me handsome. At the ball, women would be so excited in my presence that they'd leave behind small wet patches when they rose from their seats.

(Bristol returns.)

BRISTOL: By the way, I prefer Poussin's earlier version of *The Arcadian Shepherds*, in which the figures have a sense of movement, drive, a hunger for knowledge.

Spontaneity. This one is lifeless. Senator, you borrowed the wrong version.

(Bristol leaves.)

DE WOLFE: Tell me her name! Do you hear me?!

(De Wolfe waits but Bristol does not return.)

Scene Two

PROJECTED TEXT: PASSAGE OF SKIN.

The tavern. Cranston sits on the floor in great pain. Bristol stands nearby watching, seemingly unmoved by his pain.

CRANSTON: Go home. This is no place for you. It's all dregs here—

BRISTOL: You raped my mother?

CRANSTON: Aye. I did. And I'd the fuckin' gall to hope she still might run away with me. I'd buy her a pretty cottage in Lisbon, and the wages from sailing—

BRISTOL: The wages from slaving.

CRANSTON: I'd bring home to the both of you. *(Beat)* I was there at your birth. I was the one who first washed you.

BRISTOL: You will never be my father.

(Cranston muffles a sharp pain in his leg.)

CRANSTON: Jesus on the cross. The bitch wants out?! She'll tear me in two!

BRISTOL: My mother should have killed you. *(Calmly)* You'll die alone.

CRANSTON: I don't expect anything less.

(Bristol produces her knife. We're not sure what she might do with it.)

You'll butcher me?!

BRISTOL:

> The human dress is forged iron,
> The human form a fiery forge,
> The human face a furnace sealed,
> The human heart its hungry gorge.

(Cranston hears this, then lets out a short and brutal scream as the worm tries to leave his body.)

CRANSTON: Cut it. Cut it out of me!

(Bristol, after a moment, puts the knife down near Cranston so he can do it himself. Then Bristol leaves. Cranston takes the knife and makes a long cut down his leg. The worm is set free. We see the worm crawl from Cranston's leg, across the stage and then vanish. Cranston's body sags. He seems completely emptied.

Lights up on another area of the stage. De Wolfe stands alone. There is a knocking. He thinks it's the door. Then the knocking comes again, stronger.)

DE WOLFE: Who's there? *(Beat)* I knew you'd be back again. Welcome. Come in.

(De Wolfe waits for someone or something to enter. Behind him, a small hole appears in the center of the painting. Then it gets larger. A large worm appears in the hole. De Wolfe does not see it. The worm slides into the room. After a moment, De Wolfe gasps as the creature enters his body. Then he itches himself. The itch gets stronger and stronger.

Lights out on De Wolfe.)

Scene Three

PROJECTED TEXT: PASSAGE OF USEFUL LABOR.

Dembi, Nesbitt and Gifford at the docks. Gifford has died and is lightly wrapped for burial. Dembi seems caught up in thought.

NESBITT: What are you waiting for? Put him in the water. Let him sail! I'm going to make a formal complaint.

DEMBI: Listen carefully to Dembi and follow this tar's example: if you aren't dead by sundown, I kill you myself.

NESBITT: Almost dead. I hear death's tiny scratchin' in my head like a mouse. Squeak, squeak. And my brain's the cheese.

(Bristol appears. Dembi and Bristol eye one another.)

BRISTOL: What was my mother like?

DEMBI: It's not safe for you on these docks.

BRISTOL: Tell me.

NESBITT: Tell her.

DEMBI: There's an English ship in port sails in three days. You be on it.

BRISTOL: Was she pretty?

NESBITT: A sweet little gadget?

DEMBI: Pretty? Sweet? Ha. Puny words. Hard to keep my eye away, Adjua's so beautiful. She spit at every man who come near her. She could shout to cut fog. And smart? Adjua could say a word and it be a compass. And she could write. *(With joy and defiance)* Not a minute goes by—all my life—without Adjua in it. *(Beat)* You're free. Your mother gave you that. So don't waste it here.

(Dembi takes off a kente cloth that once belonged to Adjua and gives it to Bristol.)

This was your mother's. Now go back to England. Live.

(Bristol doesn't want to ask, but she can't help herself.)

BRISTOL: When did my . . . Did my mother know . . . ?

NESBITT: That you were born a—

DEMBI: Born? Born got nothing to do with it. One night, Adjua finds out the truth and she isn't disappointed. Then she can't get enough, always hankering after Dembi, my Monday. After they caught me on the docks, returned me to my master, he made me wear a dress again for seventeen years, 'til I escaped another time and come back here. In a dress, you just can't climb and duck and roll the way you have to. Adjua, she knew that being is not about what you're born, not about what you seem or speak. Who you are is what you carry. That's what she taught me. No one make Dembi. Dembi, he makes himself.

BRISTOL: That's what I need to do.

DEMBI: You're already made.

BRISTOL: No. I'm not.

(Dembi fishes some coins from his pocket.)

DEMBI: Take these coins and go home.

(Bristol won't take the coins.)

BRISTOL: How many slaves have you helped to freedom?

NESBITT: Thirty-two slaves Dembi help to freedom! Always braggin' on it. Thirty. Brag. Thirty-one. Brag. Thirty-two—

DEMBI: I make sure those running can rest before they move on to the next safe spot.

(Bristol considers his work.)

BRISTOL: I'll stay then. And work with you.

DEMBI: No. We don't even like each other.

NESBITT: I like her.

BRISTOL: Did you know her name? My aunt's name?

DEMBI: Adjua never spoke it. Not even to me. She was afraid it might be stolen—

(Dembi breaks off when Bristol takes out the book.)

That's Adjua's book.

BRISTOL: She wrote her sister's name a hundred times between the lines of William Blake. Do you want me to tell you her name?

(Dembi nods yes. Bristol leans in to Dembi and says the name. Nesbitt leans to listen, too, but he's too far away. We don't hear the name either. Dembi quietly takes it in.)

NESBITT: I mighta heard that!
DEMBI: Shut up or I'll wrap you up with Gifford.

(Bristol presses the book gently to Dembi's chest. Dembi receives the book.)

A hundred new worlds rising, that's what your mother dreamed you to be. *(Beat)* But that still don't mean you can stay and—

(When Bristol says the word "Father," she doesn't miss a beat.)

BRISTOL: So, Father. Where do we begin?

(The only emotion Dembi feels, he keeps hidden deep. Dembi eyes Bristol a moment.)

DEMBI: Take hold of this body. Help me secure the ropes.

(Together Bristol and Dembi secure the ropes around the wrapped body.)

Let's get him in the water.

(They carry the body and put it in the water. As the body sinks into the water, we hear the snapping of sails catching in the wind. The sound of sails rising. Then the spirits of Adjua, Balthazar, Liverpool Joe, and finally Cranston appear, as their younger selves. The Shadow also appears. Bristol and Dembi don't see the ghosts but they feel their force. It is now as though the dock has become their ship.)

ALL: Ready to sail!

DEMBI AND BRISTOL: Aye!

BRISTOL: I am no longer drowned.

ALL: Ready to die?

DEMBI, BRISTOL, ALL: Aye!

END OF PLAY

Further Reading

The Liquid Plain was largely inspired by the groundbreaking work of a number of historians and social critics, as well as by firsthand accounts from those whose struggles helped build the modern world.

Andrews, William L., ed. *Six Women's Slave Narratives.* New York: Oxford University Press, 1988.

Black British Former Slaves: Olaudah Equiano, Julius Soubise, Francis Barber, Cesar Picton, George Africanus, Mary Prince, Ottobah Cugoano. Memphis, TN: General Books LLC, 2010.

Blake, William. *William Blake: The Complete Illuminated Books.* New York: Thames & Hudson, 2000.

Castronovo, Russ. *Necro Citizenship: Death, Eroticism, and the Public Sphere in the Nineteenth-Century United States.* Durham, NC: Duke University Press, 2001.

Cugoano, Quobna Ottobah. *Thoughts and Sentiments on the Evil of Slavery and Other Writings.* New York: Penguin Books, 1999.

Du Bois, W. E. B. *Black Reconstruction in America, 1860–1880*. New York: Simon & Schuster, 1995.

Giddings, Paula. *When and Where I Enter: The Impact of Black Women on Race and Sex in America*. New York: William Morrow, 1984.

Hunter, Tera W. *To 'joy My Freedom: Southern Black Women's Lives and Labors After the Civil War*. Cambridge, MA: Harvard University Press, 1998.

James, C. L. R. *The Black Jacobins: Toussaint L'Ouverture and the San Domingo Revolution*. New York: Vintage Books, 1963.

Jarrell, Randall, ed. "William Blake: The Mental Traveller," in *Randall Jarrell's Book of Stories: An Anthology*. New York: New York Review Books, 2002.

Kelley, Robin D. G. *Freedom Dreams: The Black Radical Imagination*. Boston: Beacon Press, 2002.

Kelley, Robin D. G. *Race Rebels: Culture, Politics, and the Black Working Class*. New York: The Free Press, 1994.

Makdisi, Saree. *William Blake and the Impossible History of the 1790s*. Chicago: University of Chicago Press, 2003.

Rediker, Marcus. *The Slave Ship: A Human History*. New York: Viking, 2007.

Said, Edward W. *Orientalism*. New York: Penguin Books, 2001.

Wheatley, Phillis. *The Collected Works of Phillis Wheatley*. Edited by John C. Shields. New York: Oxford University Press, 1988.

PHOTO BY GREGORY CONSTANZO

NAOMI WALLACE is a playwright from Kentucky. Her plays have been produced in the United Kingdom, Europe, the United States and the Middle East. *One Flea Spare* was incorporated in the permanent repertoire of the French national theater, the Comédie-Française. Her films include *Lawn Dogs*, *The War Boys* and *Flying Blind* (cowritten with Bruce McLeod). Awards include two Susan Smith Blackburn Prizes, the Joseph Kesselring Prize, a Fellowship of Southern Writers Drama Award, an Obie Award and the Horton Foote Prize for Promising New American Play. She is also a recipient of the MacArthur "Genius" Fellowship and a National Endowment for the Arts development grant. In 2013, Wallace received the inaugural Windham-Campbell Prize for Drama, and in 2015, an American Academy of Arts and Letters Award in Literature.